PALACE OF INDUSTRY, 1851

THE VIEW OF THE PALACE FROM KENSINGTON GARDENS DOWN KING'S ROAD
BY ROBERT CARRICK

PALACE OF INDUSTRY, 1851

A STUDY OF
THE GREAT EXHIBITION
AND ITS FRUITS

BY

C. R. FAY

CAMBRIDGE
AT THE UNIVERSITY PRESS
1951

CAMBRIDGE UNIVERSITY PRESS
Cambridge, New York, Melbourne, Madrid, Cape Town, Singapore,
São Paulo, Delhi, Dubai, Tokyo, Mexico City

Cambridge University Press
The Edinburgh Building, Cambridge CB2 8RU, UK

Published in the United States of America by Cambridge University Press, New York

www.cambridge.org
Information on this title: www.cambridge.org/9780521166232

© Cambridge University Press 1951

First published 1951
First paperback edition 2010

A catalogue record for this publication is available from the British Library

ISBN 978-0-521-66123-2 Paperback

TO
MY GRANDCHILDREN

CONTENTS

LIST OF PLATES

Plate I is by the permission of proprietors of *Punch*. Plates II, III, V, VIII, IX, X, XII, XIII, XV, are by the permission of the proprietors of the *London Illustrated News*. Plate VI is from a photograph by W. E. Kilburn. Plate VII is by courtesy of Edinburgh University Library.

ILLUSTRATIONS IN THE TEXT

The illustration on page 6 is reproduced by permission of the proprietors of *Punch*. The rest are by permission of the proprietors of the *London Illustrated News*.

PREFACE

I acknowledge with gratitude the gracious permission of H.M. the King to make use of material in the Royal Archives.

I also thank the proprietors of *Punch*, *The Times* and the *News Chronicle* for help in my researches, together with the *Dalhousie Review* (Nova Scotia), in which portions of Chapters V and VI were published in 1947.

CAMBRIDGE   C. R. FAY
1 *May* 1950

CHAPTER I

ROYAL COMMISSION

'Talking of Exhibitions[1], World Fairs, and what not', said the old gentleman, 'I would not go round the corner to see a dozen of them nowadays. The only exhibition that ever made or ever will make any impression upon my imagination was the first of the series, the parent of them all, and now a thing of old times— the Great Exhibition of 1851, in Hyde Park, London.'

How came it to be?

It was announced when the distribution of prizes was made by H.R.H. Prince Albert at the Society of Arts in June last that the Society hoped to be enabled to organize a great exhibition of manufactures in 1851. We have reason to believe that since that time His Royal Highness as President of this Society has been actively engaged in devising an exhibition which shall worthily represent the present manufacturing position of the country. We hear that it is contemplated that, for the first time in the annals of similar institutions, this exhibition shall not be national only, but as far as possible, universal, embracing the products, machinery and manufactures of our country, our colonies, and all nations. It is proposed to give large money prizes and medals, which shall be awarded by a tribunal so elevated above all the interests of competition as to inspire the utmost confidence. The whole undertaking is in some way to have a national sanction to it, but the taxation of the country is not to be called upon to provide funds.

Few of the readers of *The Times* (price with a supplement, 5*d.*) who studied this news item on the morning of Monday, 27 August 1849, fully realized its implications. None knew of the Crystal Palace. Few foresaw the immense public success—at home and abroad—that would make 1851 into an almost legendary occasion, to which structures like the Eiffel Tower still bear silent homage.

[1] Thomas Hardy, 'The Fiddler of the Reels', in *Life's Little Ironies*.

1

What lay behind the newspaper announcement? How was the Great Exhibition born? The idea of exhibitions of manufactures was not new. Indeed, like so much else, it came from the France of the Revolution. The first official Exposition in the Temple of Industry had been held in Paris in 1798, the second in 1801, and others at intervals until the eleventh in 1849. These were officially sponsored. In Britain similar exhibitions had been suggested from time to time. On this occasion it was a private body, the Royal Society of Arts, which took the initiative.

The Royal Society of Arts, which flourishes still, was founded in 1754 by the drawing master, William Shipley. To it, among other things, the England of to-day owes many of its great woods, for it gave the impetus to the planting, at the lowest estimate, of fifty million trees, of which twenty million were fir and larch and fifteen million oak. Its method of premiums was commended by Adam Smith in the penultimate paragraph of his scathing chapter on Bounties (*Wealth of Nations*, bk. IV, ch. v; ed. Cannan, II, 24). Among its members was Arthur Young, who won its Gold Medal, and for a time was the Chairman of its Agricultural Committee; he said of it in retrospect in his *Annals of Agriculture*: 'It is probable that the Kingdom has benefited a thousand pounds for every guinea that has been expended.'

In 1843, when the Prince Consort became its President, the Society was rather in the doldrums; for it had failed to secure a firm footing in the stream of mechanical invention which was running so powerfully in the industrial Midlands and North. It could reward a Henry Greathead for his lifeboat, and other smaller figures for a piece of life-saving apparatus, for a fire-escape ladder, or for helmets and gauze masks to be used in the dangerous trades. (In all probability there was inspirational contact here from John Julius Angerstein, the Lord Keynes of that day, who spared time from the insurance market and from teaching Pitt how to borrow in the funds, for the humanities—the protection of chimney sweeps and other victims of industrial exploitation, and the collection of the pictures that formed the nucleus of the National Gallery.) Nevertheless, there was no doubt that the Society had drifted into a backwater. The Prince Consort was a German with an orderly and scientific mind, and he gave it the outlook needed for the embodiment of a great idea.

The reputation of public men has its ups and downs, and the Prince Consort's is just emerging from a spell of depression. Writing to Lord Granville, Prince Albert wrote as follows about a proposed statue to himself:

I can only say with perfect absence of humbug that I would much rather not be made the prominent feature of such a monument . . . as it would disturb my quiet rides in Rotten Row to see my own face staring at me; and if (as is very likely) it became an artistic monstrosity, like most of our monuments, it would upset my equanimity to be permanently ridiculed and laughed at in effigy. [Rather] mark the corners of the building [*sc.* the site of the Crystal Palace] by permanent stones, with inscriptions containing ample records of the event; and give the surplus money to the erection of the Museum of Art and Science.[1]

It was cruel luck that upon his death the Albert Memorial was erected in defiance of his wishes and with just the consequences which he foresaw.

ERECTED BY PUBLIC SUBSCRIPTION, ORIGINALLY
INTENDED TO COMMEMORATE THE INTERNATIONAL
EXHIBITION OF 1851. NOW (ALAS!) DEDICATED ALSO
TO THE MEMORY OF THE GREAT AUTHOR OF THAT UNDERTAKING
THE GOOD PRINCE

Such was the inscription proposed in July 1862, in language as ornate as the fatuous ornamentation of the Memorial itself, which in time became a target of ridicule, second only to the Albert Hall. 'The Alps indeed!' said Mr Meredith in a tone of amused pity. 'The dear girls would liefer look at the Albert Hall.'[2]

The researches of modern writers like Mr Fulford have been kinder to Prince Albert. Nor will any student of the Royal Archives sneer at him. For in them there is testimony from statesmen, scientists and men of affairs to a man of vision, discriminating, high-minded, gifted with administrative ability—and a man who could enjoy a joke as readily as we of 1950. An

[1] Royal Archives: Exhibition of 1851, vol. F25.
[2] Lady Butcher, *Memories of George Meredith*, p. 109.

undertaking like the Great Exhibition was admirably suited to the Prince Consort's energy and talents.

The idea of a Great Exhibition in Britain, however, was not his. It was Henry Cole's, a Prince Consort on a lowlier plane. Cole it was who, when the Houses of Parliament were burnt down (1834), salvaged the public records and organized the Public Record Office. He was indeed a great public servant. This done, he put himself behind Rowland Hill's campaign for the penny post. After it had been won in 1840, he battled for the standard railway gauge and cheap rates on railway parcels traffic. When finally in 1845 he was given the Royal Society's Silver Medal for a utility tea-service (or service 'for common use', in the language of the day) to be exhibited in the Society's rooms, he was marked down as the right-hand man of the Exhibition; and in 1851, the Exhibition year, he served as the Society's Chairman of Council. Like Albert, Cole has, until recently, not had his due recognition. His taste was for administrative centralization, and part of the political unpopularity which dogged him is perhaps due to the fact that, like Prince Albert, or Dalhousie of the Railway Commission, or Edwin Chadwick of the Board of Public Health, he never understood the rooted objection to it of Parliament and the English public. Thus this pioneer of industrial design and technical education was eventually to find himself forced out of public life by political opposition, barely consoled by the delayed grant of a K.C.B. (1875). We, however, can pay unstinted tribute to his efforts.

It is fair to say that without Cole and the Prince there would have been no Great Exhibition of 1851. Yet here was more than the brain-child of two able men. In the economic history of this country the Exhibition came at just the right time. For a generation Britain had moved towards Free Trade. Three years after the repeal of the Corn Laws, the repeal of the Navigation Laws in 1849 removed the last bulwark of Protection, and the majority of industrialists were prepared for foreign competition. For British business opinion, there-fore, the Exhibition was part of the triumph of Free Trade; support for it was due precisely to confidence both in the Manchester School and in the ability of British industry to meet any competition. Conversely, continental opinion was much less enthusiastic. Indeed, in 1849, the admission of products from other countries to the French Expositions had been proposed by the French Ministry of Agriculture but rejected in view of the prevailing industrial distress and unemployment in that country. Louis Napoleon, however, and the group of free-traders and St-Simonians who surrounded him, provided allies for the British champions of the Exhibition. And this country was, therefore, able to go ahead without encountering any insuperable French opposition.[1]

Britain, then, had no hesitations. Some time in 1849, with the Prince's endorsement, the decision was taken to make the Great Exhibition an international exhibition. In Cole's autobiography there is the facsimile of a minute, corrected in the Prince's handwriting, which runs:

> While it appears an error to fix any limitation to the productions of Machinery, Science and Taste which are of no country, but belong to the Civilized World, particular advantage to British Industry might be derived from placing it in fair competition with that of other Nations.[2]

Thus conceived, the Exhibition was too large an affair to be sponsored by a voluntary body. Under the circumstances the main problem was to find the best means of associating public and Government with the undertaking. It was not an easy one. Protectionists in Parliament were hostile to a Free-Trade enterprise, provincial businessmen to centralization in London, and all Englishmen to Government interference. Cole's solution was the appointment of a representative Royal Commission. As he wrote to the Hon. C. B. Phipps, 16 July 1849:

> The first step of all operations is to obtain the stamp of nationality to the Great Exhibition by means of the Royal Commission. The Society of Arts cannot begin any collection of funds until it can point to the Royal Commission as the guarantee for the proper expenditure of them. No time whatever is to be lost if anything like

---

[1] As early as 1849 Lord Normanby, British ambassador to France, saw Louis Napoleon, who favoured the idea of an exhibition and suggested that the criterion of manufactures exhibited should be 'general utility'—thus as between Babbage's calculating machine and Davy's safety lamp, the latter should win because it saved human life. Royal Archives: Exhibition of 1851, vol. F 24.

[2] The minute was adopted at a meeting at Buckingham Palace, 30 July 1849. Royal Archives: Exhibition of 1851, vol. F 8.

£100,000 is to be raised before 1851. At the present time manufacturers are thriving and making money and would be likely under these pleasant circumstances to subscribe liberally.[1]

'PITY THE TROUBLES OF A POOR YOUNG PRINCE'

(The device of a Commission had been in Cole's mind before July 1849, and he had explained it at length to Phipps on 3 July.)[2]

A combination of careful diplomacy and the support of some enthusiasts

[1] Royal Archives: Exhibition of 1851, vol. F24.　　　　[2] See Appendix II.

allowed the Exhibition to go ahead in spite of the initial reluctance of the public to subscribe. As *Punch* joked in 1850:

THE PRINCE'S PETITION
Pity the troubles of a poor young Prince
Whose costly scheme has borne him to your door;
Who's in a fix—the matter not to mince—
Oh help him out, and Commerce swell your store!
This empty hat my awkward case bespeaks,
These blank subscription lists explain my fear;
Days follow days, and weeks succeed to weeks,
But very few contributors appear.[1]

In the end a guarantee of £50,000 from some large contractors—Thomas Cubitt, Morton Peto and others—helped the project across the rapids. Eventually it did not even prove necessary to sub-contract the whole enterprise, and the original agreement to do so was revoked.

Nevertheless, political difficulties remained, none the less real because they found expression in such apparently superficial debates as those on the exact location of the Exhibition, the nature of the building that was to house it, or the prices of entry tickets.

Radical and free-trader, high Tory and protectionist, generally (but not invariably) linked, thus fought out their battles. For the Exhibition stood not merely for an economic but also for a political concept.

Lord Bloomfield reported from St Petersburg that passports were being refused to many persons of rank and station but artisans got them easily and were on their way. 'The whole affair I believe to be an attempt of the Russian Government to throw discredit on the objects of the exhibition.'

W. Temple wrote from Naples that it was feared 'the Exhibition will afford a pretext for the assembling of all the violent republicans in Europe and that the Neapolitans by mixing in such society would run great risk of having their minds tainted with revolutionary doctrines'. Paris and Vienna warned of the arrival of mischievous characters. 'I wish you joy', said Prince Schwarzenberg, 'of the select society from Vienna which you are about to

1 *Punch*, vol. XVIII, January-June 1850, p. 224.

have in London.' The Courts of Germany were canvassed for police detectives, and a Mr Eberhardt was recommended as knowing *every* suspicious character in that country.[1]

In much the same spirit of outraged Conservatism, the egregious Colonel Sibthorp, M.P. for Lincoln and chief opponent of the Exhibition, feared the irruption of foreigners, pickpockets and Socialists.

Three years after the revolutions of 1848 such fears might be quite legitimately felt. As we shall see, the fact that the Queen could move freely among great crowds in the Exhibition was regarded as a major triumph for the British political system. Certainly it was originally proposed to exclude the public from the gala opening. The ban had been lifted only under considerable public pressure, as Lord John Russell explained to the Prince (19 April 1851):

I observe that the enemies of the International Exhibition, who are not a few, are taking advantage of the recent order [denying admission to the public] to stir up discontent. Unreasonable, and indeed absurd, as this discontent is, it will be well not to let it grow. The fashionable society in London might be disregarded but it would be a pity to alienate the manufacturers and the middle classes.[1]

But the Crystal Palace was, in the minds of its supporters, not only a place where, unlike the Continent, sovereign and people could meet without the intervention of armed guards. It was also, and above all, a symbol of Free Trade and Peace: words which were regarded as almost interchangeable. Again and again do contemporaries harp on this point:

Many extraordinary trees have been grown, and are flourishing in the Chatsworth conservatory [wrote *Punch*]; but the tree of trees to be planted is the gigantic olive that is expected to take root in the Paxton Palace of Hyde Park; an olive strengthened, sheltered and protected by the glass walls and roof that admit the commercial trophies of all the world—a veritable Peace Congress, manufactured by the many-coloured hands of the whole human family.[2]

And again (for in the service of peace no pun is too atrocious):

---

[1] Royal Archives: Exhibition of 1851, vol. F 24.
[2] *Punch*, vol. IX, July–December 1850, pp. 157 and 265.

The Crystal Palace may be looked upon as a noble temple of Peace, where all nations will meet by appointment under the same roof, and shake each other by the hand. It is very curious that one half of Mr Paxton's name should be significant of Peace. We propose, therefore, that over the principal entrance there be erected in large gold letters the following motto, so that all foreigners may read it as a friendly salute on the part of England:

PAX(TON) VOBISCUM[1]

Peace and international understanding through Free Trade: the Crystal Palace was in a sense a monument to the apostles of Manchester, Richard Cobden and John Bright, little though their supporters sympathized with some of Prince Albert's more distant plans.

With political passions thus aroused, no wonder that the debates were fierce. Opponents of the Exhibition chose their ground well. If the inhabitants of Belgravia objected to the risk of seeing ordinary people in their neighbourhood, good Radicals objected no less strongly to any interference with Hyde Park, where the Exhibition was to be held.

Lord Brougham, old and crotchety, was opposed to it.[2] *Punch* fought a series of engagements against it. Thus it printed a sketch of a prison-like roundhouse (suggestive of Bentham's Panopticon) with a bell-shaped tower, on which is a white cross, and at its side a tall smoking chimney. In front a few diminutive figures are creeping towards the entrance. This was to represent 'A simple design for the proposed building in Hyde Park humbly submitted by THE ARCHITECT'. This was followed by a cartoon of 'a certain good Queen interceding with a certain Prince for the unhappy Belgravians and other citizens'.

In the end it was touch and go whether Parliament would sanction the site. All of a sudden, on 4 July 1850, the sky cleared. Let us step momentarily outside the pages of *Punch* and listen to Sir Theodore Martin. He is quoting

---

[1] *Punch*, vol. IX, July-December 1850, pp. 157 and 265.

[2] 'We are told that a Company is on foot for the purpose of buying up Lord Brougham. The object of the purchase is to send in the Hon. Lord at the forthcoming exhibition of 1851. With his Lordship the Company feels sure of winning the great prize, as there is scarcely a thing that he does not know something of; and if they can only keep him from talking, they feel persuaded they can palm him off as the most wonderful specimen of British industry.' *Punch*, vol. XVIII, p. 133.

from a letter by Prince Albert to Stockmar, written from Buckingham Palace, 3 July 1850:

Peel closed his eyes last night about eleven!! You will have heard that he fell with or rather from his horse, opposite our garden wall last Saturday, and broke his collar bone and shoulder blade. . . . Only a few hours before his accident, he was seated with us in the Commission, advising as to the difficult position into which we had been thrown by the refusal to allow us the use of the Park. . . . We are in deep grief; added to which, I cannot conceal from you that we are on the point of having to abandon the Exhibition altogether. We have announced our intention to do so, if on the day the vast building ought to be begun the site is taken from us. Peel was to have taken charge of the business in the Lower House. It is to come to the vote tomorrow, and the public is inflamed by the newspapers to madness.[1]

In her Journal the Queen wrote:

July 3. Our grief is unbounded at this national misfortune. What a making. It seems impossible yet to realise the extent of this loss to the country, and to us, and it will only be really felt in some time. In 3 days our excellent Sir Robert Peel has been snatched from us, just at a moment too, when he would have been of such use, just when my beloved one is surrounded by worries and troubles. Sir Robert had spoken so strongly about the Exhibition only 3 hours before his fatal fall,—and had advised the report being made and said *he* would hold very strong language on the subject in the House,—that the H^{se} of C. were after all a very timid body. . . . All the lower and middle class realise that they have lost a father and a friend. . . .

Sir Theodore's comment (and he was, of course, familiar with the contents of the Queen's Journal) is:

It is impossible to say how much the vote of the House of Commons may have been influenced by its being known that the voice of its most distinguished member, now silent, would have been the first to be raised in support of the appropriation of the space in Hyde Park to the purpose; but when the decision came [on 4 July] the opposition were defeated by a very large majority. In the other house the hostile motions were withdrawn and a few days afterwards the Prince was able to note in his diary, 'The feeling respecting Hyde Park is quite changed.'[2]

The shouting was over, and it remained only to build.

[1] *Life of the Prince Consort,* vol. II, p. 290.
[2] Ibid. vol. II, p. 297.

PLATE I

SPECIMENS FROM MR' PUNCH'S INDUSTRIAL EXHIBITION OF 1850

PLATE II

THE ROYAL COMMISSIONERS [I]

(L. TO R.)   LORD ROSSE, *President of the Royal Society*;
RICHARD COBDEN, ESQ., M.P.;   THE RIGHT HON. W. E. GLADSTONE, M.P.

(L. TO R.)   THOMAS BAZLEY, ESQ.;   SIR STAFFORD NORTHCOTE;
OWEN JONES, ESQ., R.A.

(L. TO R.)   DR ROYLE, *Indian Commissioner*;   WILLIAM EDMOND LOGAN, ESQ.,
F.R.S., F.G.S., *Canadian Commissioner*;   FRANCIS FULLER, ESQ.

(L. TO R.)   HENRY COLE, ESQ.; CHARLES WENTWORTH DILKE, ESQ.;
MATTHEW DIGBY WYATT, ESQ.

(L. TO R.) E. RIDDLE, ESQ., *United States Commissioner*; M. GABRIEL KAMENSKY,
Imperial Russian Commissioner;   WOLDEMAR SEYFARTH, LL.D., *Saxon Commissioner*

(L. TO R.)   DR STEINBEIS, *Commissioner for Stuttgart & Wurtemburg*;
SIGNOR CARLO TREBBI, *Roman Commissioner*; M. DUFRENOY

PLATE IV

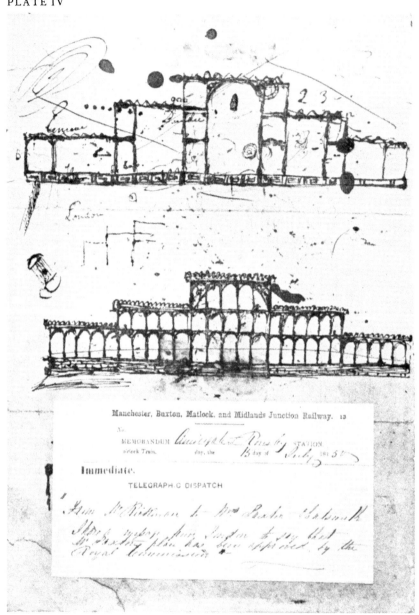

PAXTON'S ROUGH SKETCH ON BLOTTING PAPER; 'I HAVE A MESSAGE'

CHAPTER II

THE BUILDING OF THE PALACE

THE Exhibition had been prepared; now it had to be built. It is only just to let the hero of this part of our story speak for himself and at some length—for to the public Joseph Paxton, architect of the Crystal Palace, was the very embodiment of the Exhibition. Here is Paxton's own description of how the Crystal Palace came to be built, from the *Daily News* of 7 August 1851:[1]

You are aware that as soon as the Royal Commission was formed, gentlemen were selected as a building committee; to this committee was deputed the onerous duty of devising a proper building for the Exhibition. Their first public act was to send out invitations for designs for a suitable structure. About 240 designs were sent in; but the committee, not finding any of these exactly in accordance with their views, set about devising a plan of their own; and on this being completed, they prepared detailed drawings and specifications for the purpose of obtaining tenders. The structure they proposed to erect was severely commented on in the public journals on account of the vast amount of bricks that would be used in its construction, and the permanent character of the work. It was not until this war of words was raging with great fierceness that the thought occurred to me of making a design which would obviate all objections. Fortunately at this time I was erecting a house of peculiar construction, which I had designed for the growth of that most remarkable plant, the Victoria Regia; and it is to this plant and to this circumstance that the Crystal Palace owes its direct origin. Being in London, and having to see Mr Ellis, the member for Leicester, on business connected with the Midland Railway, I sought him at the Houses of Parliament, and found him at a morning sitting in the new House of Commons, which was held there on that day for the purpose of testing its fitness for use. Sir Charles Wood was addressing the House; but not a word of what he said could be heard in the Speaker's gallery; upon which I observed to Mr Ellis that I feared they would make a mistake in constructing the

---

[1] From a speech at a banquet in his honour, in Derby.

Great Exhibition Building, and that I had some thoughts of sending in a design that would solve the difficulties complained of. After a little further conversation Mr Ellis went with me to the Board of Trade to see Lord Granville. We did not find his lordship within; but Mr Henry Cole, one of the executive committee, happened to be there. I went to No. 1 Old Palace Yard, and after conversing some time with Mr Cole, I found that the building committee had advertised that the plans and specifications for contractors to tender to would be ready in about a fortnight, and I also heard that the specifications would contain a clause by which those who tendered might also tender for designs differing from the plan of the building committee. From this moment I decided that I would prepare plans for a glass structure, and the first thing I actually did was to go to Hyde Park and step over the ground to ascertain the extent in length and breadth on which the building was to stand. Having made an engagement to be at the floating of the third tube of the Britannia bridge, I could not commence the plan till after my return; and it was at the Midland station, in this town [sc. Derby], in one of the committee rooms, that the first mark on paper was made of the Crystal Palace; and the most remarkable part connected with the Crystal Palace is, that the blotting paper sketch indicates the principal features of the building as it now stands, as much as the most finished drawings that have been made since. In nine days from the time of making the blotting paper sketch, I found myself again at Derby, with a roll of plans under my arm on my way to London. These plans, five in number, had, with the exception of one, been prepared by me at Chatsworth; the one not prepared there had been made for me by Mr Barlow, the eminent engineer of the Midland Railway, who kindly gave me his valuable assistance in calculating the strength of the columns and girders. At the Midland station I had the good fortune to accidentally meet with Mr Robert Stephenson, who had come from Newcastle by the same train in which I was going to London. On our journey I showed the plans to Mr Stephenson and got him to read the specification. He expressed his unbounded admiration of the design, and promised to lay the plans before the Royal Commission on the following day, which promise he fulfilled. As Lord Brougham had said much in the House of Lords against a brick building being erected in Hyde Park, I waited upon his lordship and explained to him the nature of my plans. From that day Lord Brougham has never uttered a word against the Exhibition building, but on the contrary his lordship became my warmest supporter. I also showed the plans to Lord Granville before they went before the Royal Commissioners; and here I must remark that to Lord Granville the country owes much in respect of the success of the Exhibition. The easy access and courtesy of manner displayed by his lordship to all who approach him, added to most excellent business habits, has removed many difficulties that would not otherwise have been effected. After my design had been laid before the Royal Commissioners, and had been investigated by the building committee, and seen at Buckingham Palace by Her Majesty and Prince Albert, I took the plans to New-street, Spring Gardens, and had the good fortune to find Mr Fox at his office. Mr Fox was much pleased with the design, and at once agreed to go heartily into it. Mr Henderson (Mr Fox's partner) and Mr Robert Lucas Chance, the great glass maker at Birmingham, were telegraphed to be in London early on Monday, and after a long consultation my plans were sent to Birmingham for the purpose of having detailed estimates and drawings prepared. The Royal Commissioners were made aware of the fact of Messrs Fox and Henderson's intention to tender for my design, and Mr Cole went to Birmingham to counsel Messrs Fox and Henderson to tender for covering the ground in the exact roof as marked out by the ground plan prepared by the building committee. Mr Brunel also suggested that the interior columns should be placed 24 feet apart instead of 20, in order to suit the Exhibition. During the preparation of these plans and estimates, Messrs Fox and Henderson came to Chatsworth to settle with me some of the more important details, and I went twice to Birmingham to see the progress of the plans and estimates. During the preparation of the plans Mr Henderson suggested the transept; to this I at first objected; I did so on these grounds—namely, that as the Exhibition was to be a fair competition of skill for all nations, I held it to be right and fair that each exhibitor should have an equal advantage as regards position—which they could not have with the introduction of the transept; another objection I entertained was that it could not stand in the centre of the building as the ground plan was then arranged; but the moment Mr Henderson said it would impart strength and solidity to the building I assented to its introduction. At length the day for sending in the tender came, but considerable delay took place before it was finally accepted. I have before stated that in order to get the tender in it was necessary the building should cover the exact space marked out by the building committee; but in conforming to this plan the transept was obliged to be put into one side of the building, for the purpose of avoiding the great trees which now stand within it, but which according to the tender sent in were to be an open court. At one of the meetings of the building committee it was suggested by them that the transept should include the great trees; but there appeared at first sight a good deal of difficulty in accomplishing this, as at that time all the roofing was designed to be flat. We promised to see what could be done before the next meeting of the committee. I went direct with Mr Fox to his office,

13

and while he arranged the ground plan so as to bring the trees into the centre of the building, I was contriving how they could be covered. At length I hit upon the plan of covering the transept with a circular roof, similar to that of the great conservatory at Chatsworth, and made a sketch of it, which was copied that night by one of the draughtsmen, in order that I might have it to show Mr Brunel, whom I had agreed to meet on the ground the next day. Before nine o'clock the next morning Mr Brunel called at Devonshire House and brought me the heights of all the great trees; in the note containing the measurements, Mr Brunel wrote thus: 'I mean to try and win with our plan, but I have thought it right to give your beautiful plan all the advantages it is susceptible of.' I then showed Mr Brunel the plan I had made the night before, for covering in the trees, with which he was much pleased. I have been led into these minute details; first, to show that the circular roof of the transept was designed by myself, and not by Mr Barry, as currently reported; secondly, to show the kindness and liberality of Mr Brunel. . . . . As soon as my design had been accepted, it was decided by the Royal Commission to entrust the superintendence of its construction to Mr William Cubitt, the President of the Civil Engineers' Institute, and Messrs Fox and Henderson had, as contractors, to submit the detail drawings respecting the strength of the building for his approval.

Paxton's glass building took the country by storm:

We all know the hubbub that you, Mr Paxton, have so magically hushed [wrote *Punch*]. Our Park was to be desecrated—torn from us . . . . And then—Joseph Paxton came. And the Prince clapt his hands and said—'Paxton, go forth into Hyde Park, take glass and iron, and—beauty wedding strength—produce the Industrial Hall of Nations!'[1]

And again:

Your Glass Garden of Eden at Chatsworth; where flourish palms without rattle-snakes; and sugar canes with no yellow fever. Your Glass Palace for the Industrial Congress of All Nations; where the world will come to school (leaving their swords and bayonets at the door) and all the world learn of one another. Your Glass Houses of Parliament (that *must* be) in which statutes shall be made with so much light in them that, like glow worms, they will be at once known and studied by their own radiance.[1]

[1] *Punch*, 15 August 1850, vol. XIX, p. 81.

14

PLATE V

THE PALACE UNDER CONSTRUCTION

It was *Punch* indeed which gave the building its name, Crystal Palace.[1]

What's in a name? Sometimes very much. In christening it thus *Punch* found the right one and thus enshrined in language the structural device which contributed so markedly to the success of the Exhibition and which possibly prevented its abandonment at the last moment, to the grievous disrepute of England. The appellation stuck and accompanied the building to its new home in Sydenham. 'Glass House' would not have done; its associations are inappropriate. Nor 'Glass Palace'—that was too close to 'Gin Palace'. But 'crystal' was fairy-like and poetical. Some at first spelt it 'chrystal', but this again is wrong for 'chrystal' suggests 'chrysalis', which had nothing to do with the case. 'Crystal Palace' gets full marks.

Punch, indeed, reflects the fact that by now the whole of London was 100 per cent glass-conscious. It is proposed that the whole of London should be put under a glass cover. 'We shall be disappointed if the next generation of London children are not brought up like cucumbers under a glass.' (But would not, on the other hand, visitors to the Glass Palace swell like cucumbers in glass houses?)

A red-coated soldier was to be exhibited, ticketed, 'a lobster in crystal'. Colonel Sibthorp had been hoping that a hail-storm would hit the building. Perhaps he would throw stones himself. There was a ministerial crisis in which, after all, Parliament had to come back to the diminutive Lord John Russell, because no other foot was small enough to wear the glass slipper. There is no end to the jokes about glass.

We, as economic historians, however, are interested in more prosaic aspects of the Crystal Palace. It was one of the first great examples of standardized production. All the material used on the Palace was interchangeable; girders, columns, gutters, sash-bars were identical throughout. This, of course, enormously simplified the actual building operations and made it possible to run up the structure at a rate that amazed both the technical and the lay public. The firm of Messrs Chance Bros., glass-makers, who had been employed on Paxton's earlier, if smaller, experiments in glass building at

[1] *Punch*, vol. XIX, p. 183.

Chatsworth, were fortunately able to provide at short notice large quantities of glass made to an unusual dimension. Fifty years earlier such a technique of construction would have been impossible. In 1851 you could multiply in the

SECTIONAL VIEW OF THE GALLERIES

engineering field; in 1801 you could not. Interchangeability was the harvest yielded by the great machine-tool makers of the earlier industrial revolution, Boulton, Maudslay, Whitworth. This made possible uniform mass output, except of the master machines which guided the uniformity.

The very material out of which the Palace was built had its lessons both for contemporary and modern observers; as Charles Dickens's *Household Words* was quick to note:

The manufacture of plate glass adds another to the thousand and one instances of the advantages of unrestricted and unfettered trade. The great demand occasioned by the immediate fall in price consequent upon the new Tariff, produced this effect on the Thames Plate Glass works. They now manufacture as much plate glass per week as was turned out in the days of the Excise [pre-1845] in the same time, by all the works in the country put together. The Excise incubi clogged the operations of the workmen, and prevented every sort of improvement in the manufacture. They put their 'gauges' into the 'metal' (or mixed materials) before it was put into the pot. They overhauled the paste when it was taken out of the fire, and they applied their foot-rules to the sheets after the glass was annealed. The duty was collected during the various stages of manufacture half a dozen times and amounted to three hundred per cent. No improvement was according to law, and the Exciseman put his veto upon every attempt of the sort. In the old time the mysterious mixer could not have exercised his secret vocation for the benefit of his employers, and the demand for glass was so small that Mr Blake's admirable polishing machine would never have been invented. Nor could plate glass ever have been used for transparent flooring, or for door panels, or for a thousand other purposes to which it is now advantageously and economically applied.[1]

All the most modern methods of economizing labour were employed on the building, including machines for turning out sash-bars and gutters and for laying on paint and glazing. Two thousand men worked on the project, whose uncannily rapid progress was watched by great crowds. No less than 100,000 were reported in Hyde Park on 25 February 1851. The problem of lodging the artisans employed on the Palace was at times acute.

Yet it is worth remembering that this marvel of technique, in advance, as it remains, of much of the practice of the building industry in 1950, was built by many men to whom modern industry itself was as yet something new and strange. You may remember how Hardy's *The Fiddler of the Reels* develops. Ned Hipcroft, who had lost the love of pretty, weak-mouthed Caroline to Wat Ollamoor, leaves home and trudges up to London from his Dorset village:

The railway to South Wessex was in process of construction, but it was not yet opened for traffic; and Hipcroft reached the capital by a six days' trudge on foot, as many a better man had done before him. He was one of the last of the artisan class who used that now extinct method of travel to the great centres of labour, so customary then from time immemorial.

In London Ned worked at his trade:

The fourth year of his residence as a mechanic in London was the year of the Hyde Park Exhibition already mentioned, and at the construction of this huge glass-house, then unexampled in the world's history, he worked daily. It was an era

[1] *Household Words*, no. 54, 1 February 1851.

17

of great hope and activity among the nations and industries. Though Hipcroft was, in his small way, a central man in the movement, he plodded on with his usual outward placidity.

It was the meeting of the world of Ned Hipcroft and of the American McCormick reaper at the Exhibition of 1851 which gives that year its peculiarly historical flavour.

A smaller building was going up side by side with the Palace. Prince Albert insisted on erecting a set of model working-class dwellings as near the Exhibition as possible—in the grounds of Knightsbridge Barracks. It was one of the few efforts in connexion with the Great Exhibition to remember the working population of Great Britain. At least one man, Charles Dickens, appreciated the Prince's intentions and satirized his opponents:

It is an infamous fact, sir, that all these things—these five rooms and a closet leading out of the lobby—are specially so contrived that they can be let to tenants at a weekly rent of four shillings and sixpence.[1]

By the aid of banter wholehearted praise was given to the Prince's contribution to the housing problem.

One last problem might, perhaps, be mentioned. We shall let another architect of the Great Exhibition, Lyon Playfair, tell the story, for he is a good raconteur:

The Prince Consort was in the breakfast-room at Buckingham Palace, moody and unhappy, when the Queen asked the cause of his woe. He explained that after innumerable difficulties had been removed, the sparrows had appeared in such numbers in the Exhibition as to destroy all hope of displaying valuable goods. The Queen then asked whether the Prince Consort had consulted Playfair, and was assured that he had no advice to offer. Thereupon she suggested that Lord John Russell should be sent for. On his arrival at Buckingham Palace, the Prince Consort explained the difficulties in regard to the sparrows, and his lordship at once suggested that Her Majesty's Guards should be sent into the building to shoot them. The Prince pointed out that this was an unpractical suggestion, as the result must be that the palace of glass would be destroyed. Lord John Russell then suggested that Lord Palmerston should be called into consultation. When the great

---

[1] Mr Bendigo Buster on the Model Cottages, *Household Words*, no. 67, 5 July 1851.

statesman arrived he smiled at the difficulty, and proposed that birdlime should be put on the branches of the trees. The Prince Consort observed that this proposal was equally useless, because the sparrows no longer roosted on the trees, but preferred sitting on the iron girders of the building. Lord John Russell and Lord Palmerston now withdrew for a consultation, and finally recommended that the Duke of Wellington should be summoned. A messenger was accordingly despatched to Apsley House, and found that great warrior and statesman in the act of leaving home for the Horse Guards. The Iron Duke was annoyed at being summoned for such an object, and wrote the following letter: 'Field-Marshal the Duke of Wellington presents his humble duty to Her Majesty. The Duke of Wellington has the honour to be Commander-in-Chief to her Majesty's Forces, but the Duke of Wellington is not a bird catcher.' The Duke had no sooner sent the letter than he repented, and, mounting his horse, overtook the messenger, and, taking back his letter, presented himself at Buckingham Palace. The Queen received him with effusion, and the Prince Consort recovered from his despondency. The three Privy Councillors withdrew for a consultation, and on their return the Duke of Wellington oracularly uttered the word 'Sparrow-hawks'. In the meantime the sparrows had sent out scouts. When they heard that Lord John Russell had been summoned they twittered, and seemed to be amused. When Lord Palmerston went they showed signs of anxiety, but ultimately flew about as usual. When their scouts informed them that the Duke of Wellington had gone to the Palace, all the sparrows congregated in the tree nearest to the door, and as soon as the advice of sparrow-hawks was communicated they flew in a body out of the door, and the Exhibition was never again troubled with their presence.[1]

Lyon Playfair takes this story, he says, from a provincial journal. He does not, however, suggest that it was based on fact.

While the Palace is being built, let us see how the approach of the Great Exhibition struck contemporaries. There can be no better guide than the series of news items and progress reports in the *Daily News*, a Liberal paper, which was a strong supporter of the Exhibition from the outset. For the Exhibition was, as we have seen, superb testimony to the Free Trade for which the paper stood. *The Times* is not so good a guide, for it was both hostile to the Consort and badly off the mark in its estimate of the Exhibition's success. In July 1850 it had prophesied a deficit of £85,000 ('our calculations

---

[1] Wemyss Reid, *Memoirs and Correspondence of Lyon Playfair*, 1899, pp. 119-20.

may be relied upon'), a prophecy which supporters of the Exhibition took care to recall gleefully. Nor, incidentally, was Charles Dickens's forecast of the Exhibition's success much better. Though a good friend to the Exhibition, even in July of 1851 he had misgivings about the result:

I have always had an instinctive feeling against the Exhibition, of a faint, inexplicable sort. I have a great confidence in its being a correct one somehow or other—perhaps it was a foreshadowing of its bewilderment of the public. My apprehension—and prediction—is, that they will come out of it at last, with that feeling of boredom and lassitude (to say nothing of having spent their money) that the reaction will not be as wholesome and vigorous and quick, as folks expect.[1]

The *Daily News*, however, had no hesitation. Let us join its middle-class readers, and watch, in mounting enthusiasm and pride, the progress of the great work. On 1 January 1851, we hear of the first preliminary classification of exhibits. And then news titbits. The descendants of the Pilgrim Fathers are sending their exhibit to the very port from which their ancestors were driven by persecution in 1620. Embroidered shawls and ivories have arrived from India by the overland mail via Alexandria. Messrs Fox and Henderson, contractors, held a gathering of the Royal Society, to which Professor Cowper demonstrated the lightness and strength of the building. On 2 January we read an advertisement asking for tenders for refreshments: ices, pastry, sandwiches, patties, tea, coffee, chocolate, cocoa, lemonade, seltzer and soda water; bread, butter and cheese, chocolate, ginger beer, spruce beer. A few days later the paper reports that Mr Charles Gilpin and other advocates of the Temperance Movement have addressed a letter to Prince Albert complimenting him on the exclusion of intoxicating drinks from the Exhibition refreshment rooms, and hoping that His Royal Highness had not sanctioned the late distribution of beer among the workmen engaged on the building. Other sections of the public were not so enthusiastic about this decision.

---

[1] Dickens to W. H. Wills, 27 July 1851, from Broadstairs, Kent—in Walter Dexter, *Letters of Charles Dickens*, vol. II. Dickens, a Londoner through and through, forgot the industrial Midlands and North. Hard times to him were marvellous times to them. And they thronged to see the machines at work about which they would talk for the rest of their days.

On 14 January we hear that Liverpool is to send a model of its port, and models of vessels, including the Atlantic steamships of the Cunard (British) and Collins (American) lines: samples also of all its imports. A firm of hairdressers (!) advertises a Great Exhibition Almanack in English, French and German, with cab fares and a six-day guide.

By 17 January (when there is a noisy meeting about the registry of interpreters and guides) we find what we have been looking for all along. Advertisements begin to show the influence of the coming Exhibition. Thus: 'What lamps will gain the prize?—The best are Clark's Lamps for certain....' The tone of the Exhibition is set by two items on 18 January: an engraving of the interior of the Crystal Palace, and the Report of the Manchester Committee, which answers numerous businesslike queries. Solid business is combined with gorgeous spectacle. A few days later Thomas Miller of Edinburgh makes a remarkably close forecast of attendance at the Exhibition:

Visitors, foreign and Colonial	2 million
— United Kingdom . .	5 million
Railway receipts, accruing from the Exhibition traffic . . .	£4.7 million

To meet this influx (it is reported on 4 March), a Joint Stock Association is now in course of formation in Belgium. It is intended to purchase a line of steamers capable of carrying 250 passengers each and run them so as to make three trips a week.

By April the *Daily News* is jubilant:

Difficulties have thawed away. Nothing remains but to reiterate the hope we have so frequently expressed, that in the spirit wherein they began they will continue steadfast to the end, knowing no distinction of persons, of nations, or of opinions, but contributing by the most splendid of instructive displays to convince the world of the folly of its long-cherished jealousies, animosities, and exclusions.

Meanwhile the life of the country was going on. Parliament was in session and Lord John Russell's ministry was tottering from crisis to crisis. Maybe, but for the impending Exhibition, Stanley would have put it out forthwith.

There were enormous debates on the Budget and the Papal Disabilities Bill. The taxes on knowledge (stamp duty, advertisement duty, paper duty) were anger spots, and although they would have gone one day in any case, the atmosphere of the Exhibition with its appeal for the support of the populace was an argument in favour of their repeal. Macready, the actor, retired from the stage. There was uproar at the meetings of railway shareholders ('Let us have a dividend! Who cooked the accounts?'), and outside Europe there was the sensational growth of San Francisco and the Californian gold rush.

And now the race for the Exhibition was entering its last lap. On 17 April the *Daily News* begins to print the list of exhibitors in seven or eight columns per issue, continuing over the next seven days. By 28 April the painters are out, the scaffolding is removed, the canvas blinds are fitted. The packing-case debris has been cleared away. On 1 May the doors would be opened at 9 a.m. and closed at 11.30 until the departure of the Queen.

And then came the great day of opening. Only the Corps Diplomatique failed to share in the general enthusiasm and refused to present an address at the opening ceremony. 'I am afraid they are making great fools of themselves', wrote the Prince to Lord John Russell.[1]

It had been the Prince's idea to associate them formally with an international proceeding in which all nations had taken an active part: 'Half the building was in charge of foreign authorities, half the juries were appointed by foreign governments who have also defrayed the expenses of the foreign part of the Exhibition.' Thus the Prince defended the proposal to Palmerston, but as it was declined, the scheme had to be dropped, and the outcome was that the diplomatists would attend only as spectators and on future occasions have places reserved whenever the Queen was formally present.[1]

What were a handful of diplomatists among the enthusiastic crowds? Dickinsons' *Comprehensive Pictures of the Great Exhibition of 1851* almost drowns in the waves of sonorous prose with which it attempts to describe the great occasion:[2]

[1] Royal Archives: Exhibition of 1851, vol. F 24.
[2] *Dickinsons' Comprehensive Pictures of the Great Exhibition of 1851* (2 vols.), 1854.

Brilliant and solemn was the spectacle which is depicted in the accompanying plate. An assemblage composed of the magnates of England, and of Continental Europe, of the aristocracies of birth, of intellect and of wealth was 'waiting for the Queen'. The talented orator astounding Parliament with his eloquence, the wily diplomatist playing with the destinies of Empires, the illustrious in war, in literature, in science, and in art, were gathered together upon that platform 'waiting for the Queen'. Around them and above them a girdle of female beauty, such as even the glowing pencil of a Sir Peter Lely would have failed to depict, encircled the building from north to south, and from east to west. The Englishwoman, calm in the possession of her chaste and aerial loveliness, the animated Parisienne, rich in her indescribable grace, and the daughter of the South, with her restless and impassioned gaze—each and all contributed their charms to lend enchantment to the scene.[1]

The Exhibition was open. All the world hailed it, none more fervently than the correspondents of Queen Victoria:[1]

Lord John Russell to the Queen: 1 *May*

Everything went off so well that it is needless to mention particulars, but the general conduct of the multitudes assembled, the loyalty and the content which so generally appeared were perhaps the most gratifying to a politician; while the wonders of Art and Industry will be the most celebrated among philosophers and men of science, as well as among manufacturers and the great mass of the working people.

The Archbishop of Canterbury [in reply to the Queen's message of thanks]:

It will always be a pleasing reflection that a part was assigned me in a ceremony which afforded such unmixed gratification to a multitude of H.M.'s subjects.

Edward Kater [who had been seated opposite to the throne]:

We have never witnessed such a scene in the history of the world. Most justly may the Prince be proud of to-day! It seemed more like the realization of the thoughts of the poet or painter, or some delightful fairy tale. The continuous cheering . . . as H.M. and the Prince moved along the Procession, was very exciting.

The Chinese Commissioner insensibly touched with the solemnity of the scene, during the Hallelujah Chorus, taking his way slowly round the margin of the fountain and making a prostration before H.M.—and as not less touching to me

[1] Royal Archives: Exhibition of 1851, vol. F 24.

the old Duke, taking the arm of the venerable Marquis of Anglesea and both insisting upon going the whole way round in the Procession. The appearance of the Prince of Wales in his pretty Highland dress and the Princess Royal with her wreath of roses looking so sensible. . . .

CLARENCE HOUSE, 1 May 1851

My beloved Victoria,

That was indeed a most glorious day and sight. I saw many people crying in seeing you together with your children. . . . I wish you both joy, particularly dearest Albert who has so much to do.

I felt so nervous and anxious yesterday and this morning, and *now* I feel very happy and pleased.

Pray give a kiss to that gracious little boy of yours,

Ever your most affectionate Mother.

The Duchess of Gloucester to the Queen:

. . . I am rejoicing that the foreigners should have witnessed the affection of the people to you and your family, and how the English people do *love* and respect the *Crown.*

Palmerston to the Queen [after telling her that Oporto had declared for the insurgents]:

. . . the event of yesterday, a day the result of which must be not less gratifying to Your Majesty than honourable to the nation whose good fortune it is to have Your Majesty for its Sovereign.

The King of the Belgians (Uncle Leopold) to the Queen: 5 *May* 1851

I am glad foreigners saw for once, that to the highest authority in the state even a great and free country like England may show real and great respect. The sceptical and cynical turn which the Press in France has given to the public mind has shown itself since the Restoration by constant efforts to render the supreme government, and particularly the person ostensibly at the head of it, ridiculous and odious in every way: they have very pretty results to boast of this system.

The Queen to Lady (Sarah) Lyttleton:

The ceremony was most touching and beautiful. To see this great conception of my beloved husband's great and good brain—which is always labouring for the

24

good of others—to see this great thought and work crowned with triumphant success, in spite of difficulties and opposition of every imaginary kind and sort, and of every effort which jealousy and calumny could resort to, to cause its failure, has been an immense happiness to us both—but to me the glory of his name, united with the glory of my dear country, which shone more than she has ever shone, on that day—is a source of pride, happiness, and thankfulness which none but a wife's heart can comprehend. The sight of the Crystal Palace was indescribably glorious, really like fairyland. The Exhibition itself is of an extraordinary interest, and highly instructive. . . . We pay it many visits.

Little Arthur received a visit from the old Duke on his birthday.

Finally, there is a letter from the Embassy in Turin, adverting to the admiration of people there 'for the institutions and government of a country, where, without risk to the public tranquillity, such an undertaking had been possible of execution'—'an inspiration to liberalism'.[1]

And in this first week of May 1851, with a feeling for publicity not usual in a close corporation, the Provost and scholars of King's College, Cambridge, informed the Vice-Chancellor of their University, who informed the press, that 'We, being desirous of establishing a more perfect system of equality and unity of interest with the said University . . . do hereby relinquish all right and title whatsoever to be exempt from the ordinary examination of the University...'. Restriction was breaking down before the wave of Liberalism, even in its last strongholds.[2]

---

[1] Likewise in the solid prose of the *Kölner Zeitung*: 'Man muss es gestehen, dieses Werk könnte nur in England vollbracht werden.'

[2] Within a year the number of matriculations at King's doubled—one freshman in October 1850, two in October 1851.

CHAPTER III

SOME LEADING ARCHITECTS

THOMAS HARDY contends that 1851 was 'a precipice in time'. If this is so it is profitable to watch those who bestrode it—not merely or mainly those to whom it came towards the end of a career moulded in a previous age, such as Wellington, Palmerston and Lord John Russell, but rather those who, having made their mark before 1851, crowned it with work in a wider theatre. I think of Richard Cobden moving from Corn Law Repeal in 1846 to the French commercial treaty of 1860, of Gladstone advancing from the Board of Trade and railway regulation to the Exchequer and his great Free Trade budgets, and of the many other great and less great Victorians who made the Exhibition what it was. Prince Albert and Henry Cole we have already mentioned. But there are other men who embodied in their different ways two vital aspects of the Exhibition, the practical and the scientific.

First and foremost comes Joseph Paxton (1801-65).

'Arise, Sir Joseph' (23 October 1851). As the Queen wrote in her Journal for 15 October, 'an immense, though deserved distinction . . . . He was only a gardener's boy'.

Born and bred near Woburn, Beds, he went up to London and became a foreman in the Chiswick Gardens of the Royal Horticultural Society. There the Duke of Devonshire, in residence at Chiswick House, met him, and in 1826 made him his head gardener at Chatsworth. Within ten years Paxton had made its garden and himself well known. For he was not only a great practical gardener, but also a horticultural writer of some merit, launching in turn a Horticultural Register and a Magazine of Botany. Thus it was not ducal patronage alone which caused him to be associated with the public inquiry into the state of the Royal Garden of Kew in 1838.

The Report, printed in 1840, is by Dr Lindley, Professor of Botany, who at the request of the Treasury 'made an actual survey of the Botanical Garden at Kew, in conjunction with Messrs Paxton and Watson, two practical gardeners'. They found a state of congestion and scientific neglect—the great Botany Bay house overcrowded, with its magnificent specimens from New Holland and elsewhere, unnamed: no liaison with the colonies or with scientific institutions at home: the ground decently cultivated but used mainly to supply the royal establishments with floral decorations.

'The most wealthy and most civilised kingdom in Europe offered the only European example of the want of one of the first proofs of wealth and civilisation.' Dublin and Edinburgh had their public botanical gardens, but not the metropolis. 'Medicine, commerce, agriculture and horticulture, and many valuable branches of manufacture would derive considerable advantages from the establishment of such a system.' Royal ownership had, indeed, prevented the land from falling to the speculative builder, but now it should be bought by the nation: 'It is inconceivable that Parliament would refuse the money to a garden so remodelled.'

This recommendation was the beginning of the changes by which, under the direction of Sir William Hooker and his son Joseph Dalton (Huxley's lifelong friend), Kew became the great institution of our own day, an imperial as well as a national asset. All know the story of the Hevea seed sent out from Kew Gardens, which was the foundation of the rubber industry of Ceylon and Malaya. (The changes at Kew from 1838 to 1872 are detailed in a Parliamentary Paper, no. 47 of 1872.)

Gardening and botany: what is their place in the records of an island empire?

An Englishman's home was not a castle, nor had it been for several centuries, but a house with grounds in the privacy of which he performed all manner of feats, classical, romantic and utilitarian. Sir Willoughby had a laboratory as well as a leg. The itch for improvement, which eventually spread throughout the British economy, had its origin here. Gardening became a hobby, and the sight of a stately garden was to its owner a perennial joy. What a seneschal or major-domo did in the old days, I have never clearly visualized, but whatever his duties were, I conceive him to have lived in the back premises. The head gardener was different. He had his own little house and garden, and the great garden was a dyarchy shared between master and servant, though in the case of Angus McAllister, head gardener to the ninth Earl of Emsworth, it was not always clear who was the master. But the good head gardener was attached not only to his employer but to his garden even more —to his pumpkin or his lily, as the case might be. When, therefore, Paxton, after his work for the Kew Commission, was offered the post of royal gardener at Windsor, he had no difficulty in refusing the honour. The Duke did not need to write post-haste, 'Paxton, come back, MUSA CAVENDISHII needs you'.

Thus much on the domestic side. But Chatsworth was more than a private house. It throws light on the contribution of the British aristocracy to imperial economy. In the course of two centuries, say 1651-1851, we had risen to pre-eminence not indeed in shipbuilding, but in seamanship and seafaring. Trade carried the flag, and science was in the ship's company on the *Endeavour*, the *Beagle* and the *Rattlesnake*. Revolve the noble Exhibition globe, housed now with the Royal Geographical Society, and point if you can to a sea where the White Ensign had not fluttered! The world was scoured for specimens of animal and vegetable matter from wild beasts to monkey puzzles. With James Cook on the *Endeavour* went Sir Joseph Banks, President of the Royal Society, whose collections enriched the British Museum. And there were similar treasure hunts in the life of Paxton and the bachelor Duke, culminating in a tragedy in the quarter of the world where Cook also perished. For after a successful expedition to the East, which yielded *Amhersta nobilis*, a new and marvellous tree with splendid geranium buds, from the borders of Burma and Assam, the Duke financed, and Paxton organized, a similar expedition to the West, with the help of Sir William Hooker and John Lindley, sometime assistant librarian to Sir Joseph Banks. The Hudson's Bay Company helped the expedition, which was led by two young gardeners from Chatsworth, across Canada, but disaster overtook it in the rapids of the Columbia River, and the leaders perished, the news reaching home in May 1839. 'Only a gardener's boy', but, twelve years before 1851, well known to the world of scientific exploration.

As economists we distinguish between the extensive and intensive margin. In a broad sense the extensive margin is set by the explorer, and the intensive margin by the inventor. Both are concerned with the finding of novelties, of things that exist elsewhere, and their transplantation. Invention itself in its early stages is bound up with ransacking the brains of others and imitating their performance. There was piracy in the workshop as well as on the high seas. But Paxton as an inventor borrowed only from himself, and his greatest invention was the Crystal Palace, which was a new way of making, on an unprecedented scale, something imperatively demanded by the emergency of the moment. And it had this mark of a great invention—it was fully adequate to its purpose. This history of invention is littered with misfits and follies, and the Crystal Palace housed some such, but it was not itself one of them.

The sequence by which Paxton reached his great idea is a familiar story (which, after it had been told in *Household Words*, vol. ii, no. 43, 18 January 1851, most of England knew by heart)—first the Great Conservatory at Chatsworth, then the Lily House, then the Crystal Palace. The Lily House was built on the ridge-and-furrow principle:

> Perfect facilities for drainage and ventilation were required. For this the new house provided that the roof was not only a roof, but a light and heat adjuster; the iron columns were not only columns but drain pipes; rafters and sash bars served the same purpose. The floor was not only a floor but at the same time a ventilator and a dust trap. Multiply these principles in a building covering not sixty feet but eighteen acres, weld glass and iron together by girders above and below, and what emerges is—the Crystal Palace.[1]

Yet in the Victorian Paxton a passion for the technical side—whether of gardening or engineering—inevitably merged with the enjoyment of private enterprise, the urge for profits.

[1] V. R. Markham, *Paxton and the Bachelor Duke* (1935), pp. 181-2.

There was no reason why a ducal gardener should be a railway 'fan', but so he was, and even more was his wife, Sarah. Violet Markham, Paxton's granddaughter, was brought up in Tapton House, Chesterfield, the house, now a school, in which was held recently the centenary celebration of George Stephenson, who died there in 1848. Paxton was the close friend of both the Stephensons, and he accompanied the father on his last continental tour in 1846. The fireman's son and the gardener's boy received a royal welcome everywhere, and the gardener contrived that they should see also the best waterworks in each place.

In the eighteenth century few escaped the smallpox. In the nineteenth few, with the means of indulging it, escaped the railway fever; and, as with cigarette-smoking to-day, the women were as susceptible as the men. 'A railroad!' exclaimed Tancred, with a look of horror, 'A railroad to Jerusalem!' But unlike Disraeli's Lady Bertie, Mr and Mrs Paxton were on the side of the narrow gauge, which was the Stephenson gauge, and they did well out of it:

Mrs Paxton to her husband:

How I wish I could have been in the City to-day. Shares are horribly low, and I am looking out for a line to have a bit of a private go.

And again (September 1845):

My dearest and best,

In the supplement to the *Railway Chronicle* I found a very satisfactory report of the Birmingham and Gloucester directors....The Bredbury call is due to-day.... I see in the paper a prospectus of the Southern Manchester and Oxford Junction Railway. Is it a limb of the great one or an opposition one?... There has been a perfect tribe at Chatsworth to-day. I hope I shall hear from you in the morning. Goodbye, God bless you and protect you. . . .

What a helpmeet! For while Herbert Spencer had to extract his father from a rash investment in 'Middies', Sarah steered her spouse through the shoals, and she was not taken in by George Hudson. But Paxton, having become a director of the Midland Railway of which Hudson was chairman, retained a kindly memory of the Railway King, seeing that the King, before his collapse, purchased for a handsome figure the Duke of Devonshire's

PLATE VI

SIR JOSEPH PAXTON

PLATE VII

SIR LYON PLAYFAIR

Yorkshire estates, which had to be sold to meet the lavish outlays at Chatsworth.

After 1851 Paxton, now Sir Joseph, continued his life of restless activity. He represented Coventry in Parliament, 1854-65, and as their member had to find arguments against Cobden's damaging treaty of 1860. He fitted out a Navvy Corps for the Crimea, joining *The Times* in the fight against official incompetence. He was consulted on exhibitions at home and abroad, he planned a grander London, and he entertained lavishly at Rockhills, his Sydenham house, at which the Duke of Devonshire (until his death in 1858) was a frequent visitor. A house in Bedfordshire near to the place where he had been employed as a gardener's boy was his last building contract. He was buried in Edensor churchyard, Derbyshire, near the man he had loved and served, near the man who wrote of him, 'To me a friend, if ever man had one'.

If Paxton represents the empirical side of the Exhibition, Lyon Playfair (1818-98) represents the scientific and intellectual.

Professor of Chemistry at Edinburgh University, 1858-69, he was the grandson of Principal Playfair of St Andrews, and himself reared in academic circles. At Glasgow he had for classmate David Livingstone,[1] and a second was James Young, the founder of the paraffin oil industry. But his most valuable contact was at Giessen with Baron von Liebig, whose great work he translated into English—'*Organic Chemistry in its Application to Agriculture and Physiology;* By Justus Liebig: edited from the manuscript of the author by Lyon Playfair, 1840.'

The banner of the decade was Public Health, its tragedy the Irish Famine, and with both Playfair was associated. His first public work was as a Royal Commissioner on the State of Large Towns (1844-5), and he reported on Lancashire because he had been employed there as a chemist to a Clitheroe print works and also was honorary Professor of Chemistry to the Royal

---

[1] Livingstone, who to the Oxford British Association meeting of 1860 sent a letter from River Shiré, 4 November 1859, 'On the Latest Discoveries in South Central Africa', concluding: 'There are thousands needing Christian instruction, and there are materials for lawful commerce and a fine healthy country. Let but a market be opened up for the purchase of their cotton, they can raise any amount of it, and the slave trade will be effectively abolished'—which puts in a nutshell the economic imperialism of mid-Victorian England.

Institution at Manchester. His reputation there was such that the venerable John Dalton attended his lectures, and Peel already thought so highly of him that he intervened to dissuade him from accepting a chair at Toronto. In December 1844, he writes to Prince Albert: 'I have some very distinguished men here [Drayton Manor]. . . .Dr Lyon Playfair [the translator of Liebig], Professor Wheatstone [the inventor of the electric telegraph], Professor Owen of the College of Surgeons, Mr George Stephenson, the engineer.' Later Playfair and Wheatstone were neighbours at Hammersmith, and so alike facially that on one occasion Lady Wheatstone mistook Playfair for her husband; and they amused themselves on their Sunday walks by deciphering the cypher advertisements in *The Times*.

Professor Owen was Sir Richard Owen (1804-92), the Hunterian Professor of Comparative Anatomy, and the *D.N.B.* epitome says of him: 'Devised models of extinct animals at Crystal Palace; as superintendent of natural history collections of the British Museum obtained their separation from the library and removal to South Kensington (1881), where he designed the "Index Museum".'

In December 1845 Peel writes again to the Prince: 'The accounts from Ireland in the month of October, from the Lord Lieutenant, from the constabulary, from the men of science whom we sent there to investigate, Dr Lyon Playfair and Dr Lindley, the first chemist and first botanist, were very alarming. The worst account was from the men of science.'

In 1845 Playfair came to London to serve under Sir Henry de la Beche in the new School of Mines in Jermyn Street, and in 1850 received an invitation from Lord John Russell to become a 'Special Commissioner' and a member of the Executive Committee for the management of the Exhibition. Under pressure from Peel, who had previously made him known to the Prince, and on condition that he should be free to consult Peel at every turn, he accepted; for no one knew the manufacturers' minds as Peel did. And the consultations were frequent down to the morning of the day of Peel's fatal accident, 29 June 1850. In the preparations for the Exhibition Playfair's special duty was to prepare the classification, which, as he tells us, he did by dividing manufactures into 29 classes, each of which was subdivided into subsections, representing the distinct industries. The classification was empirical, but the manufacturers understood it and co-operated heartily. In the proceedings of the Exhibition his principal task was to superintend the awards of the juries, which consisted of men of all nations, half the appointments being British and half foreign. He was thus the liaison officer of the Exhibition. He kept the provinces in line with London; he arbitrated on jury disputes, and being both on the Commission and the Executive Committee, he was the mediator between the two. Henry Cole, the mainspring of the Executive Committee, was not an easy man to work with, but Playfair gained his confidence, and eliminated the friction that had threatened to develop between Commission and Committee.

With the closing of the Exhibition Playfair's work for the 1851 Commission had in fact only begun. He served it for 45 years, 1850-95, being a formal member of it from 1869 and its honorary secretary, 1882-9. In 1855 he became Secretary of the Science and Art Department. His contribution to it may best be summed up in two quotations from the *Memoirs*:

The central feature of the Prince's scheme was the establishment of a practical institution for the application of science and art to productive industry. This was the beginning of the two great institutions, one being known as the South Kensington and now as the Victoria and Albert Museum, and the other as the Royal College of Science.[1]

If to Sir Henry Cole belongs the credit of having placed the Art Department upon the lines on which it was successfully developed, to Playfair no less belongs the honour of having given form and substance to that part of the scheme which was specially related to the establishment of a national system of scientific instruction.[2]

Sir James Dewar, the Jacksonian Professor of Natural Experimental Philosophy, was a pupil of Playfair, and writing to the widow from the Royal Institution of Great Britain, 31 May 1899, he said: 'He was my master in everything, and I owe all to him. If he had only been spared a little longer,

---

[1] *Memoirs*, p. 141.   [2] Ibid, p. 143.

I wanted so much to have told him that at last hydrogen had succumbed, and about the new work I have in hand.' Dewar was a man not given to flattery.

In the last forty years of his life Playfair was a professor (for a period) and a politician, as well as a servant of the public. In 1858 he returned from London to Scotland, to the coveted chair of chemistry in Edinburgh University. He was already F.R.S. and an ex-President of the Chemical Society, which he had helped to found. What his backers acclaimed in him was the ability 'to expound the truths of experimental science in a clear, logical, audible, and, to me, satisfactory manner', the 'me' in question being M. Faraday. In writing 'audible' Faraday may have had in mind the inability, which some of our greatest scientists have revealed, to make themselves heard by a large audience. From the time when Francis Hutcheson and Adam Smith revolutionized the professorial lecture by speaking in the English tongue, the Scottish tradition of high-grade lecturing had held. In his inaugural lecture Playfair took as his subject 'A Century of Chemistry in the University of Edinburgh'; and after reviewing the work of his predecessors, which included Adam Smith's friend Joseph Black, the discoverer of latent heat, he accepted for himself the role of 'missionary to bring chemists in relation to the industries of the country, which had too long been carried on by the rule of thumb'.[1] When he resigned his chair in 1869, the Minutes of the Senatus paid testimony to 'his earnestness in the advancement and in the practical application of science, his admirable powers of organisation, and his efforts to obtain scholarships and endowments and to render the University more directly useful in guiding the general education of the people'.

But once a public servant, always a public servant. The first major distraction was the Exhibition of 1862, where reluctantly he took charge of the administration of awards: the second was the acrimonius Cattle Plague Inquiry of 1865. This and other public business compelled him to resign his chair in 1869, the year after he had entered Parliament as member for the Scottish Universities. In 1892 he was raised to the peerage as Baron Playfair of St Andrews, and in 1898 he died.

[1] *Memoirs*, p. 181.

In each new task he revealed the qualities of the great liaison officer of 1851. In Parliament he was a loyal disciple of Gladstone, yet being a university member he had to speak for many who were conservatives but had voted for him because of his academic standing. For some years, therefore, he intervened chiefly in educational issues and tried to present the non-partisan case. In 1885 he left academic Scotland for the working-class constituency of South Leeds, which he held by large majorities, 1885-92. This fact throws an interesting light on England in the 1880's.

For many Gladstonian liberalism was the stepping-stone to Labour politics. (One thinks of Philip Snowden's youth.) If some liberals, *nouveaux riches*, held their seats by showering wealth, others owed it to their zeal for democracy, whereby class feeling was submerged in the fervour for popular causes.

In party organization the liaison officer *par excellence* is the chief whip, who is the central link between the Prime Minister and his followers. The post was offered to Playfair in 1880, but he declined it, believing that he lacked the qualifications. However, 'soon afterwards I was offered the office of Chairman and Deputy Speaker of the House of Commons and in an unhappy hour for my own peace of mind I accepted it'.[1] It was the time of Irish obstruction, and a storm broke on his head when he suspended sixteen of the obstructionists. He had to resign, but the fairness of his decision was proved by the fact that the Irish themselves were the first to sympathize with their enemy of the moment.

Playfair, the professor, could administer. Like Henry Fawcett, the blind Professor of Political Economy in Cambridge, he held the office of Postmaster General, in those days the highest-ranking office outside the Cabinet, but owing to a change in the administration his tenure was short (1873). His second office, Vice-President of the Council, i.e. Minister of Education, was equally short (1886) and for the same reason. But he had a characteristic success. He carried, where others had failed, a Bill for the reform of the medical profession. 'By adequate firmness, combined with a spirit of conciliation, the Bill was steered through both Houses without a single amendment

[1] *Memoirs*, p. 296.

on its main principles, and by becoming law it settled the angry controversies of the medical profession.'[1]

Mr Lloyd George must have sighed for a Playfair at the birth of National Health Insurance. The power to find a solution acceptable to conflicting interests had been displayed some years previously in the Manchester Water Supply (Thirlmere) Bill:

> The Committee reported in favour of the Bill, but it took special care that the beauty of the district should be enhanced, and not deteriorated. This was easy, for formerly the lake was larger, but the water had worn away a natural dam and partially emptied itself. We gave power to restore the dam in a picturesque way, and thus increased the size of the lake. I presume that my judgment was good, for public excitement was calmed, and I have never since heard a word against our decision.[2]

Picturesque, yes, but lacking the natural blend of land and water, and rather dead, because for reasons of water purity none may prowl around its banks.

When the British Association met at Montreal under Lord Rayleigh in 1884, Playfair was present, being president-elect for the Aberdeen meeting of 1885. At Aberdeen he was back in his native Scotland, as also in spirit were many of those Canadians whose overpowering hospitality he had recently enjoyed. After Aberdeen he was a guest at Balmoral and Glamis, and so in 1887, when the Golden Jubilee of Queen Victoria was celebrated, he and other like-minded liberals—such as Lord Rosebery and Sir Charles Dilke, were asking themselves how the imperial tie might be strengthened without recourse to the retrograde policy of Protection. Some found a solution in imperial federation. Playfair hoped much from the Imperial Institute, built on the site which he had done so much to develop. If the Imperial Institute, when built, had not the scope which he designed for it, this must be ascribed in part, as in the case of Imperial Federation, to the difficulty of associating the Dominions with it on terms acceptable to themselves. Playfair was, however, the reverse of a Jingoist. Married in late life to an American lady, he made America a second home and worked ceaselessly for a good

[1] *Memoirs*, p. 360.   [2] Ibid, p. 246.

36

understanding between the British and American peoples, alike in academic and political affairs.

Where, in other countries, the aristocracy held aloof from industrial development, in Britain it threw in its lot wholeheartedly with the middle classes. The Earl Granville, 1815-91, was (after the Prince Consort) the central figure on the Royal Commission for the Exhibition of 1851 from its inception on 3 January 1850 to the end of his long political life. He owed much to his father, the first Earl Granville, 1773-1846. The Foreign Secretary inherited from the diplomatist charm of manner, felicity of diction and a familiarity with foreign tongues which greatly aided the policy of international comity. He at least would not be accused of saying in Paris 'Vous avez drivé devilish slow'. During the Exhibition he was Vice-President of the Board of Trade, and he served also as Vice-President to the Commission. He was *persona gratissima* to the Royal Family, and the correspondence to and from him in the Exhibition archives would make, if adequately edited, an entertaining monograph.[1]

As the son of an English ambassador to France, he did much by his personal influence to promote the *Entente Cordiale* between England and France, which grew steadily from that time until the time of Edward VII, who admired him and learned from him. The contribution of his tact and knowledge to the Exhibition's success is incalculable.

With him we may mention three other aristocratic members of the Royal Commission for the Exhibition of 1851: the Earl of Ellesmere, the Duke of Buccleuch and the Earl of Rosse.

The Duke of Buccleuch (1806-84) belonged to a ducal house made famous to political economy by its association with Adam Smith, and had been Peel's Lord Privy Seal. A wealthy landowner and a benefactor to Scotland, he presided over numerous societies, and finally became Chancellor of the University of Glasgow.

---

[1] One example out of very many: Ashley (the Lord Shaftesbury of social reform) had protested against the crucifix in Pugin's medieval court. Granville to Ashley, 20 March 1851: 'It wasn't a crucifix, only a cross, and Pugin had agreed to place it in a corner. He regrets the occurrence and says it reminds him of having damned an opera at Drury Lane, when his Gothic chair was turned into a Devil in the midst of a pathetic scene before Macbeth got into the Infernal Regions.'

The Earl of Ellesmere (1800-57), statesman and poet, was heir to the Duke of Bridgewater, the pioneer of canal building. An early promoter of Free Trade and that Radical foundation, London University, he became in turn President of the Camden Society, the British Association (1842), the Royal Asiatic Society and the Royal Geographical Society. In his person Manchester landed and business property was associated with the culture and learning of the Metropolis.

The Earl of Rosse (1800-67) introduces the great name of Parsons. Distinguished for astronomy and the improvement of the telescope, he was President of the Royal Society at the time of the Great Exhibition. However, the Exhibition was, above all, the work of the Victorian middle class—industrialists, merchants, bankers, engineers. The membership of the Royal Commission is a cross-section through the world of 'private enterprise' in Britain at that period.

There were the engineers: John Scott Russell (1808-82), Robert Stephenson (1803-59), and Sir William Cubitt (1785-1861).

Russell was the naval architect who constructed the *Great Eastern*, designed by I. K. Brunel (the hull and paddles being by Scott Russell, the screws by James Watt and Co.). She was a very strong ship with double bottom and tubular upper deck, but built in advance of her time. Her gross tonnage was 18,914.

Robert Stephenson, the son of the great George Stephenson, was one of the most eminent engineers of his time in his own right. His father's collaborator in the construction of the 'Rocket' and various railway lines, his best known achievement is the Menai Bridge, opened in 1850.

Sir William Cubitt, F.R.S., was a civil engineer, whose son Joseph constructed the Great Northern Railway. Peel had delayed the final list of Royal Commissioners till January 1850, when William Cubitt, as the new President of the Institution of Civil Engineers, would sit *ex officio*. He had the highly important task of supervising the erection of the Exhibition building, and he negotiated the subsequent purchase of the South Kensington properties. A Norfolk boy, he had risen to the head of his profession via windmills, treadmills and agricultural implements—he was for long chief engineer at Ransome's at Ipswich. Later, as consultant first for canals and then for railways, he became the central figure in the committee rooms at Westminster. He was engineer in chief, South Eastern Railway, and in 1856 the Commissioners reported that 'Sir William Cubitt was superintending the construction of the new museum' (the Victoria and Albert to be). His breadth of mind was shown by his readiness to examine Paxton's last-minute design and in the support which he gave as soon as he had studied the detailed plans.

Industry was represented by Bazley, Gott and Gibson.

Thomas Bazley (1797-1885) stood for Cotton. A spinner from Bolton, Lancs, and prominent in the Anti-Corn Law League, he was Chairman of the Manchester Chamber of Commerce in 1851, and a member of the Mercantile Law Commission (which, incidentally, in 1854 reported against the grant of limited liability to partnerships). In 1855, after serving as a Commissioner for the 1855 Paris Exhibition, he received the Legion of Honour. He was M.P. for Manchester 1858-80 and became a baronet in 1869.

Wool was represented by John Gott (1791-1867), the head of Benjamin Gott and Sons, woollen clothing manufacturers and merchants, the great pioneers of the industry in Leeds. He was in politics a Conservative. An obituary says: 'It was not less due to his being head of the greatest woollen firm in Leeds than to his sound sense of manufacturing and mercantile pursuits that he was appointed one of the Royal Commissioners for the Great Exhibition of 1851.'

The third great textile industry, silk, was represented by Thomas Field Gibson (not to be confused with Thomas Milner-Gibson, sometime President of the Board of Trade). The Commissioners were asked if they approved of devoting the Exhibition's surplus to the purchase of the South Kensington estate, and Gibson's reply is interesting: 'Yes, provided that steps were taken to allay the provinces' fear of over-centralization. The School of Design at Somerset House was abortive, till provincial schools were started—now it has taken on a new lease of life.' (Cobden, in his reply, was so apprehensive of benefiting one country at the expense of another that he could think of nothing better than an electric telegraph connecting the eastern and western hemispheres!)

Banking and insurance provided Samuel Jones Loyd and Thomas Baring.

Samuel Loyd, Lord Overstone (1796-1883), was created a baron in 1850, and at the time of the Exhibition was president of the Statistical Society. His advocacy of the Currency Principle and its acceptance by Peel in the Bank Act of 1844 is standard economic history.

Thomas Baring (1799-1873), Conservative M.P. for Huntingdon and Chairman of Lloyds, was twice offered the Exchequer by Lord Derby, the post which his elder brother, Sir Francis Baring, had held under Melbourne. The importance of the House of Baring in the economic life of nineteenth-century Britain, and indeed the world, is too well known to require comment.

Thomas Cubitt (1788-1855) represented an older industry which was as yet by no means overshadowed by the new developments of the Industrial Revolution. He had been ship's carpenter, master carpenter and then builder, first in the parish of St Pancras (Upper Woburn Place, Gordon Square, etc.), and then in Belgravia—moving west as the building of great houses moved west,—and he built the east front of Buckingham Palace. In 1850 he, with his fellow-contractor Morton Peto (elected to the Commission 1863), and several others, put up the needed guarantee, which incidentally was repaid with interest out of gate receipts three weeks after the Exhibition opened. But his greater service was as unpaid agent for the purchase of the South Kensington estate, conducted officially by Sir William. He understood land values and knew that the purchase would add to the rising values of the neighbourhood. He is the 'our Mr Cubitt' of the Queen's Journal because, in addition to work at Buckingham Palace, he had assisted Prince Albert in laying out Osborne and its drainage system.

Agriculture finally provided, besides its noblemen, Philip Pusey (1799-1885), landlord and scholar (he was the elder brother of Pusey of the Oxford Movement), and the intimate of Peel and Gladstone. Converted to Free Trade in 1847, he was Chairman of the Agricultural Implements section of the Exhibition, and wrote the section report. He helped to found the Royal

Agricultural Society in 1838, and his zeal for tenant-right caused Disraeli to call him its father. (There is a letter from him in the Exhibition archives on the solemn subject 'Should cheeses be admitted?')

Beside the entrepreneurs, the intellectuals. Out of the great tradition of Benthamite reform came Edgar Alfred Bowring, C.B., son of Sir John Bowring, the noted Utilitarian. An official of the Board of Trade, he was Acting Secretary to the Commissioners, and Secretary to their Finance Committee, from 1850. In 1852 he was appointed Secretary to the Commission in succession to Sir Stafford Northcote (the future Conservative Chancellor of the Exchequer) and J. Scott Russell, although he had been carrying out most of the duties of that office as Acting Secretary. He held the post of Secretary for seventeen years until 1869 when he resigned to take up his duties as M.P. for Exeter, the seat to which he had been elected in the previous year and which he subsequently held until 1874. He died in 1911.

The arts were represented by Sir Richard Westmacott (1775-1856), Sir Charles Eastlake (1793-1865) and Sir Charles Barry (1795-1860): sculptor, painter and architect respectively.

To Westmacott we owe the statue of the Duke of York on the Duke of York's column and the reliefs on the Marble Arch, which in 1851 was removed from Buckingham Palace to Cumberland Gate in Hyde Park.

Eastlake, President of the Royal Academy in 1850, had been brought into contact with Prince Albert as Secretary to the Fine Arts Commission, and was henceforth chief adviser to the Prince and the Government on matters of art. The *D.N.B.* says of him: 'The cultivation of the arts in this country received so marked a stimulus from the Exhibition of 1851 that their progress since is generally and in the main rightly ascribed to its influence; but it should not be forgotten that a vigorous movement for the promotion of art had commenced long before and that the Exhibition itself was the outcome of prolonged exertions in which Eastlake was second to none.' His chief written work was *Materials for the History of Oil Painting*.

Sir Charles Barry was the well-known architect of the Reform Club and the Houses of Parliament.

The most eminent representative of the sciences was Sir Charles Lyell (1797-1875), the famous geologist and precursor of the theory of evolution.

Such were the men who built the Exhibition and who were entrusted with the task of carrying out the greater design of which it was to be part. In their strength and limitations they represent the Britain of 1851—with one great omission.

No working-men were consulted in its planning; none were represented on the Commission. Though they built the Crystal Palace and made the machines and manufactures exhibited there, few troubled even to acknowledge their work. As the poet Thomas Hood put it:

> But what to me are these inspiring changes,
> That gorgeous show, that spectacle sublime?
> My labour, leagued with poverty, estranges
> Me from this mental marvel of our time.
> I cannot share the triumph and the pageant,
> I, a poor toiler at the whirling wheel,
> The slave, not servant of a ponderous engine
> With bounding steam-pulse and with arms of steel.

Punch, it is true, was aware of the omission:

The Great Exhibition of Industry will not be complete without an addition which *Punch* proposes to make to it. An exhibition of manufactures and commodities is not an exhibition of industry, but one of the results of it. A real exposition of Industry would require that the INDUSTRIOUS themselves should be exhibited as well as their productions. In a glass hive we ought to show the bees at work. However, as needlewomen cannot be starved, nor tailors 'sweated', nor miners blown up, amongst a multitude of people, with any degree of safety, it is suggested that paintings of our various artisans labouring in their usual vocations, should accompany the display of substances and fabrics which we owe to the labours or ingenuity of the respective classes. Pictorial art might thus be brought to make appropriate contributions to the world's bazaar. Shall we ostentatiously show off all manner of articles of comfort and luxury and be ashamed to disclose the condition of those whom we have to thank for them?[1]

In its first Exhibition cartoon, indeed, the paper proposed 'Specimens from

[1] *Punch*, vol. xx, January-June 1851, p. 42.

Mr Punch's Industrial Exhibition of 1850 (to be improved in 1851)'. In this we see Prince Albert stroking his chin, as a severe top-hatted Punch presents in glass cases—an industrious needlewoman, a labourer aged 75, a distressed shoemaker, a 'sweater'.[1] (Plate 1)

But *Punch* was then still a social reformer of the sentimental order. Except among such, the products of labour held all the limelight, the labourer none. To the eye of 1951 this is perhaps the most surprising aspect of the Great Exhibition.

[1] *Punch*, vol. XVIII, January-June 1850, p. 145.

CHAPTER IV

THE QUEEN'S EXHIBITION JOURNAL[1]

BUT it is time now to visit the Exhibition. Who could be a better guide than Queen Victoria herself, who has confided all her joys and exertions to the Journal which we are to read?

1851

February 15. Albert took Queen Marie . . . to the Crystal Palace.

February 18. After breakfast we drove with the 5 children to look at the Crystal Palace, which was not finished when we last went, and really now is one of the wonders of the world, which we English may indeed be proud of. I annex some views of it. The galleries are finished, and from the top of them the effect is quite wonderful. The sun shining in through the Transept gave a fairy-like appearance. The building is so light and graceful, in spite of its immense size. Many of the Exhibits have arrived, and some from Germany were being unpacked. The test of the strength of the galleries was made on a platform, made precisely the same size, on which 250 men rushed and sprang upon it to see if the weight would be borne, a trial which the galleries never will have. We were again cheered loudly by the 2,000 workmen, as we came away. It made me feel proud and happy.

March 6. 6 young ladies from the City have presented me with a really magnificent carpet, worked by 150 ladies, for the Exhibition. We had already 10 days ago seen and admired it.

April 7. We talked of . . . the King of Sardinia's wishing to come to England for the Exhibition, which we would be very glad of. We afterwards went with the two boys to the Exhibition, which is so interesting and entertaining that I should like to go there every day. The flooring is all laid down, and the progress is immense since we were last there. Two most beautiful colossal statues, one, of a

[1] The Journal survives in the form of the fair copy made by the Princess Beatrice, to whom the Queen left it. It is believed to be a faithful transcript, though incomplete. When the Queen illustrated her journal with pen-and-ink or coloured sketches, the Princess cut them out, and they are bound into the text, so that on the reverse of these it is possible to see specimens of the Queen's own handwriting.

lion, from Munich, the other by Kiss, a Prussian, of an Amazon, whose horse is attacked by a Tiger, are up now. The wood carving from Vienna is quite beautiful. There was much French machinery, which the French themselves fear they will not shine in. Several French directors were there.

April 15. At a little after 5 I went with the 2 girls and Bessy D. to the Exhibition, where Albert had already been some time, having attended a Commission. As usual, the gentlemen attending to and superintending the works were there: Mr Dilke, Mr D. Wyatt (a very intelligent architect), Mr Fox, etc., besides Col. Reid[1] and Ld. Granville walked about with us, which we did for 2 hours. We must have walked quite six miles! The building has got on immensely. We in fact only visited a few sections, but it took so much time. The sculpture from Austria including Milan is extremely pretty.

April 18 (Good Friday). We dined alone and went to the Library ... after which we saw Col. Phipps about a difficulty that has arisen relative to the opening of the Exhibition.

April 19. Mama etc. dined, which we did rather late, Albert having had to see Ld. Granville about the great difficulties connected with the opening of the Exhibition. It was to have been in State, but a private view. *Now* the public want to be admitted and are in a great state of excitement about it. So we must try and get the matter arranged somehow.

April 21. Ld. John Russell came to see us after luncheon, and we talked principally about the opening of the Exhibition, which is to be an entirely State affair, and we shall view the Exhibition privately on the 30th.

April 28. On reaching Buckingham Palace we walked over the rooms in the new wing, which have been arranged for the P^ce and P^cess of Prussia, and which really are very nice. After luncheon we received P^ce Henry of the Netherlands who arrived yesterday. The Corps Diplomatique are to walk in the Procession at the opening of the Exhibition. Albert hastened to a Commission there.

April 29. We drove to the Exhibition with only the 2 Maids of Honour and 2 Equerries, and remained about 2 hours and ½. I came back quite dead beat and my head really bewildered by the myriads of beautiful and wonderful things, which now quite dazzle one's eyes. Such efforts have been made and our people have shown such taste in their manufactures, all owing to the impetus given by the

[1] Gen. Sir William Reid, F.R.S., 1791-1858, chairman of the Executive Committee of the Great Exhibition: 'Its punctual opening at the appointed time was in great measure due to his quiet determination. He was an ex-governor of Bermuda' ('The Good Governor' of *Household Words*, no. 23, 31 August 1850) and after receiving his knighthood was appointed, 27 October 1851, Governor and Commander-in-Chief at Malta.

Exhibition and my beloved one's guidance. We went up into the Gallery, and the sight of it from there into all the Courts, full of all sorts of objects of art, manufacture etc. had quite the effect of fairyland. The noise was tremendous, as there was so much going on, of all kinds and sorts, and at least 12 to 20,000 engaged in work of every kind. The collection of raw materials is very fine. The clocks and articles of silver, stuffs, English ribbons lace etc. are beautiful. Indeed, it shows of what immense use to this Country this Exhibition is, as it goes to prove we are capable of doing almost anything. We went down and examined the French part, in which there are most exquisite things from Sèvres, Aubusson and the Gobelin manufactures, and the most splendid arms of all kinds. Looked also at the Italian, Spanish, Portuguese and German parts. The Austrian section is nearly finished, and beautiful. There are very splendid exhibits in porcelain and iron, from Berlin, lovely embroideries from Switzerland, etc. Russia is far behind as the ships were frozen in and could not bring the things sooner. We lunched rather earlier and received M. Musurus, the new Turkish Minister, a Greek by birth, and a very agreeable man, and then Baron Koller, to present a letter from the Emperor of Austria, who gives me a beautiful carved writing table (which was at the Exhibition) containing five albums etc. Albert went to the Station to meet the P^{ce} and P^{cess} of Prussia. At $\frac{1}{4}$ to 4 they arrived and I was down at the door to receive them, and their son and daughter, afterwards taking them to their rooms. The young Prince, who is 19, is not handsome, but has a most amiable attractive countenance and fine blue eyes.

April 30. Everyone is occupied with the great day and afternoon, and my poor Albert is terribly fagged. *All* day some question or other or some difficulty, all of which my beloved one takes with the greatest quiet and good temper. We breakfasted with our dear guests and our girls, driving immediately afterwards to the Exhibition, where we walked about with the P^{ce} and P^{cess} and their son and daughter. The noise and bustle even greater than yesterday, as so many preparations are being made for the seating of spectators and there is certainly still more to be done. We walked the whole round of the galleries. We saw beautiful china from Minton's Factory and beautiful designs: there was also very fine Wedgwood ware. Below, we looked for a moment at the Turkish. The fountains were playing and many flowers and palms have been placed, which have a most charming effect.

May 1. This day is one of the greatest and most glorious days of our lives, with which, to my pride and joy, the name of my dearly beloved Albert is for ever associated! It is a day which makes my heart swell with thankfulness. We began the day with tenderest greetings and congratulations on the birth of our dear little

Arthur. He was brought in at breakfast and looked beautiful with blue ribbons on his frock. Mama and Victor were there, as well as all the children and our dear guests. Our little gifts of toys were added to by ones from the P^ce and P^cess.

The Park presented a wonderful spectacle, crowds streaming through it,—carriages and troops passing, quite like the Coronation, and for *me*, the same anxiety. The day was bright and all bustle and excitement. At ½ p. 11 the whole procession in 9 State carriages was set in motion. Vicky and Bertie were in our carriage (the other children and Vivi did not go). Vicky was dressed in lace over white satin, with a small wreath of pink wild roses in her hair, and looked very nice. Bertie was in full Highland dress. The Green Park and Hyde Park were one mass of densely crowded human beings, in the highest good humour and most enthusiastic. I never saw Hyde Park look as it did, being filled with crowds as far as the eye could reach. A little rain fell, just as we started, but before we neared the Crystal Palace, the sun shone and gleamed upon the gigantic edifice, upon which the flags of every nation were flying. We drove up Rotten Row and got out of our carriages at the entrance on that side.[1] The glimpse, through the iron gates of the Transept, the waving palms and flowers, the myriads of people filling the galleries and seats around, together with the flourish of trumpets as we entered the building, gave a sensation I shall never forget, and I felt much moved. We went for a moment into a little room where we left our cloaks and found Mama and Mary. Outside all the Princes were standing. In a few seconds we proceeded, Albert leading me, having Vicky at his hand and Bertie holding mine. The sight as we came to the centre where the steps and chair (on which I did *not* sit) was placed, facing the beautiful crystal fountain was magic and impressive. The tremendous cheering, the joy expressed in every face, the vastness of the building, with all its decorations and exhibits, the sound of the organ (with 200 instruments and 600 voices, which seemed nothing) and my beloved husband, the creator of this peace festival 'uniting the industry and art of all nations of the earth', all this was indeed moving, and a day to live for ever. God bless my dearest Albert, and my dear Country, which has shown itself so great to-day. One felt so grateful to the great God, whose blessing seemed to pervade the whole undertaking. After the National Anthem had been sung, Albert left my side and at the head of the Commissioners,—a curious assemblage of political and distinguished men—read the Report to me, which is a long one, and I read a short answer. After this the Archbishop of Canterbury offered up a short and appropriate prayer, followed by the singing of Handel's

---

[1] i.e. on the north side (and not by the main entrance on the south side facing Kensington Road).

Hallelujah Chorus, during which time the Chinese Mandarin came forward and made his obeisance. This concluded, the Procession of great length began, which was beautifully arranged, the prescribed order being exactly adhered to. The Nave was full of people, which had not been intended, and deafening cheers and waving of handkerchiefs continued the whole time of our long walk from one end of the building to the other. Every face was bright and smiling, and many had tears in their eyes. Many Frenchmen called out 'Vive la Reine'. One could of course see nothing but what was high up in the Nave, and nothing in the Courts. The organs were but little heard, but the Military Band at one end had a very fine effect, playing the march from 'Athalie' as we passed along. The old Duke of Wellington and Ld Anglesey walked arm in arm, which was a touching sight. I saw many acquaintances amongst those present. We returned to our place and Albert told Ld Breadalbane to declare the Exhibition to be opened, which he did in a loud voice saying 'Her Majesty commands me to declare this Exhibition opened', when there was a flourish of trumpets, followed by immense cheering. We then made our bow and left.

All these Commissioners and the Executive Committee etc. who had worked so hard and to whom such immense praise is due, seemed truly happy, and no one more so than Paxton, who may feel justly proud. He rose from an ordinary gardener's boy! Every one was astounded and delighted. The return was equally satisfactory, the crowd most enthusiastic, and perfect order kept. We reached the Palace at 20 m. past 1 and went out on the balcony, being loudly cheered. The P^ce and P^cess were quite delighted and impressed. That *we* felt happy and thankful, I need not say, proud of all that had passed and of my beloved's success. I was more impressed by the scene I had witnessed than words can say. Dearest Albert's name is for ever immortalised, and the absurd reports of dangers of every kind and sort, put out by a set of people—the 'soi-disant' fashionables and the most violent protectionists,—are silenced. It is therefore doubly satisfactory that all should have gone off so well and without the slightest incident or mischief. Phipps and Col. Seymour spoke to me, with such pride and joy at my beloved one's success and vindication after so much opposition and such difficulties, which no one but he with his good temper, patience, firmness and energy could have achieved. Without these qualities, his high position alone could not have carried him through. Saw later in the evening good Stockmar after having had a little walk, and he rejoiced for and with me. There was but one voice of astonishment and admiration. The 'Globe' had a beautiful article which touched me very much—I forgot to mention that I wore a dress of pink and silver, with a diamond ray diadem and little crown at the back with 2 feathers, all the rest of my jewels being diamonds. The P^cess looked very handsome and was so kind and 'herzlich'. An interesting episode of the day was the visit of the good old Duke, on his 82nd birthday, to his little godson, our dear little boy. He came to us at 5, gave little Arthur a gold cup and toys, which he had chosen himself. Arthur gave him a nosegay. We all dined 'en famille', the children staying up a little longer, and then went to Covent Garden opera, where we saw the 2 finest acts of the 'Huguenots'—given as beautifully as last year.—Was rather tired, but we were both too happy and full of thankfulness for everything.

May 2. A fine morning. After our pleasant breakfast we took our morning's walk. The papers full of beautiful descriptions, and there is but one voice of praise from all quarters for the glorious result of the undertaking. The 'Times' has some very true remarks, which I shall transcribe. 'There was yesterday witnessed a sight the like of which has never happened before and which in the nature of things can never be repeated. They who were so fortunate as to see it hardly know what most to admire,—or in what form to clothe the sense of wonder and even of mystery which struggled within them. The edifice—the treasures of art collected therein, the assemblage and the solemnity of the occasion,—all conspired to suggest something more than sense could scan, or imagination attain. There were many familiar with magnificent spectacles, many who had seen Coronation Fetes and solemnities, but they had never seen anything to compare with this.... Around, amidst them, and over their heads were displayed all that is useful or beautiful, in nature, art and science. Above them rose a glittering arch, far more lofty than the vaults of even our noblest cathedrals. On either side the vista was almost boundless. It was felt to be more than what was seen or what had been intended. Some saw in it the 2nd and more glorious inauguration of their Sovereign, some, a solemn dedication of art and its stores. Some were reminded of that day when all ages and climes should be gathered round the Throne of their Maker. There was so much that seemed accidental, and yet had a meaning that no one could be content with simply what he saw.'

At 12 we went to the Royal Academy.... After luncheon we drove in the Park with the 2 girls and past the Exhibition. There were quantities of carriages but no squeeze or inconvenience, and everyone in such good humour. What an answer is this again to that mischievous set of people, though there are many whom I know and like, who up to 12 o'clock on the night of the 30th maintained something dreadful would happen! Col. Grey is so delighted and proud of my beloved Albert.

May 3. A tolerably fair morning. Immediately after our breakfast we drove with the P^ce and P^cess, P^ce Fritz, our eldest children etc. to the Crystal Palace, where Ld Granville, Col. Reid, Mr Mayne and other gentlemen connected with the Exhibition joined us. We confined our inspection almost entirely to the plate and jewellery, on the English side, which together with clocks and watches fill ½ of one gallery. There are beautiful things amongst them. We went across in front of the great organ, to view maps, diving apparatus, and a wonderful invention of a Pole, an anatomical figure made to take the shape and size of any person. Looked down on the carriages, of which there is a handsome collection. Stopped in the Austrian Room to view the magnificent bookcase, containing the splendidly bound albums and books, sent me by the Emperor. Many things in the French section are (strange to say) not ready. The Nave being now clear of people looked beautiful, and one could admire all the works of art placed in it. There are seats placed for people to rest. During the last hour many people came in, but it occasioned no inconvenience. P^ce Fritz, who is really a most good, unaffected amiable and simple young man, took our children about, the whole time. We came back at ½ past 11, much pleased and interested, for so much knowledge was imparted to me and the use of everything etc. etc. explained, so that one really got a good deal of information. It ought to do wonders in enlightening young people, both high and low. We were much pleased with 2 drawings by Mr Nash[1] of the opening of the Exhibition, which gave a good idea of that grand scene.

May 4. A bitterly cold day. . . .The Princess and her son went with us to the Chapel, where Mr Wellesley preached a very nice sermon, alluding in a very pretty and proper manner to the Exhibition, and the good will it would lead to, if taken as it ought to be. The text was from the xviith Chap. of Acts, verse 26: 'And (He) hath made of one blood all nations of men to dwell on all the face of the earth'. Good Stockmar was with me for some time, and in the course of conversation said how my beloved one *was now* appreciated. Ld John Russell, Sir G. Grey and Sir F. Baring all saying how they looked up to him. Ld Granville had tears in his eyes, when I spoke to him yesterday and praised him, answering he had only carried out Albert's orders . . . . L^d and L^y John Russell dined. Both spoke with delight of the opening of the Exhibition, and of every circumstance attending it, as well as of its immense utility to the Country. My dearest Albert is so pleased at the realisation of what he always foretold. The Protectionists, who opposed the project of the Exhibition, are much provoked, and many who would not go, so provoked at not having been there! We looked at the beautiful albums from the Emperor of Austria.

[1] Frederick Nash, 1782-1856, water-colour painter.

May 5. I held a Council ... and saw Sir G. Grey, who gave excellent reports of the state of London, and that there had not been *one* accident on the 1st of May, nor *one* Police Report; that it had been estimated that between 5 and 700,000 people had been assembled in the Park that day! Inside the building there were between 20 and 30,000. After the Council we saw Ld Grey who could not cease praising the Exhibition, its beauty and its usefulness in every sense of the word. He had been there early this morning.

May 7. . . . to the Exhibition remaining there nearly 2 hours and being received by Ld Granville and the other gentlemen. We went to the courts allotted to Tunis and China, which are very interesting, and Tunis particularly beautiful, being arranged as a native bazaar, full of magnificent embroideries, stuffs, metal work etc., and the blending of colours exquisite. In all these compartments there are likewise the *raw* products, dried fruits, perfumery, in fact everything that can be made in each country. Fom here we crossed the Transept to where the Indian exhibits were placed. We were quite dazzled by the most splendid shawls and tissues. Next went to South Australia and New Zealand, where the exhibits consist chiefly of raw products—but very valuable ones, such as beautiful specimens of wood etc. Canada made an admirable show, fine furniture, pretty sledges, and a very good and novel kind of fire engine.[1] We then went into the Sculpture Court, containing many fine pieces including some by Bell, Thornycroft, Foley etc. After this to Mr Pugin's mediaeval room, full of church ornaments, beautiful mantle-pieces etc. and lastly through a collection of furniture, lamps, ornaments of the most novel and tasteful kind from Birmingham. This was an interesting morning's work. Enormous quantities of people, with differently priced tickets, come all and every day.

May 10. . . . to the Exhibition where we remained 2 hours. This time we directed our steps to where we left off last time, stopping however, on the way, to look at a beautiful statue by Geefs of a female figure with a lion[2] and at some beautiful jewellery by Lemonnier belonging to the Queen of Spain, also some lovely artificial flowers by Constantin. Chubb's locks were the 1st exhibits we regularly inspected, and they really are wonderful of every size and kind. He explained to us the ingenious manner by which an attempt to force the lock is discovered. Next to the Courts with furniture, which make a very satisfactory

---

[1] Cf. *Montreal Gazette*, 26 May, from its Canadian correspondent in London: 'The Fire-engine was the next article that attracted notice, and they examined it most minutely. They desired me to put it in working order that they might see it complete. To do this, the Prince most kindly gave me his assistance. We detached the hose reel and showed the Queen its use.'

[2] Catalogue—'Belgium 466: Plaster group, *The Lion in Love*, by Ch. Geefs'.

display, is the Birmingham ware, papier mâché etc. From here we made a very detailed inspection of the Sheffield ware, beginning with a model of the process by which steel is made from iron and finishing with the most beautiful cutlery. There were Bowie[1] knives in profusion, made entirely for Americans, who never move without one. Went thro' all the woollen department, with specimens of every kind and texture—the flax, linen, and cambrics from Ireland (very fine) and beautiful muslins from Glasgow. We then walked through the section containing agricultural implements, finishing up with Switzerland, where there are many specimens of embroidery and wood carving from the Oberland and musical boxes, watches etc. from Geneva. It was a most interesting instructive visit. Many of the exhibitors themselves were there, explaining their products, amongst whom Mr Hook from Sheffield, who went round with us. He was very dissatisfied, as well as many other exhibitors, at their claim to be present at the opening not having been granted. Every time one visits this great work one feels more and more impressed with its lofty conception. The mottos of the Catalogue, chosen by my beloved Albert, are very appropriate and significant of the great undertaking, such as: 'The Earth is the Lord's and all that therein is'—'The compass of the world and they that dwell therein'—'Say not the discoveries we make are our own. The germs of every art are implanted within us, and God, our instructor, without our knowing it, develops the faculties of invention'—'The progress of the human race resulting from the labour of all men ought to be the final object of the exertion of each individual. In promoting this end we are carrying out the will of the Great and Blessed God'. This latter motto is Albert's own.

May 12.... to the Exhibition. We went through the sections of raw materials beautifully arranged: minerals, ore in all shapes, coal, copper, marble, crystal etc. Professor Ansted[2] went with us, and I wish we could have given more time to this interesting section. Then we crossed over to the other side where the carriages were—of all sorts and descriptions, some very pretty—also saddlery, harness etc. Visited the locomotives, but by $\frac{1}{4}$ to 11 the building got so full we had to hurry away.

May 14. We went immediately after breakfast to the Exhibition... our visit being confined to the paper, stationery, printing and book binding department, which is very interesting and instructive. There are every specimen of printing in colours, the types, woodcuts, stereotype etc. The Fine Arts Court, containing wood carving of every kind and sort, was most beautiful. Amongst it was our

[1] Said to be named from one Colonel Bowie.
[2] David Thomas Ansted, 1814-80, Professor of Geology at King's College, London.

beautiful cradle, and a most exquisitely carved side-board, representing portions from 'Kenilworth' executed by a man of the name of Cook from the wood of an oak tree near Kenilworth. There were also enamels, medals, daguerreotypes and photographs.[1] Amongst the enamels were ours by Essex.[2] The numbers of people who visit the Exhibition are enormous, the average receipts being £2,300 a day.

May 16. ... to the Exhibition where we remained more than an hour. Visited in detail, 1st the Austrian section, where there is printing of the very finest kind, particularly coloured prints, work tools, which are very good etc. There are very fine cabinets, exquisitely worked. We again visited the rooms, which are indeed beautiful. The other products of the commercial kind require no enumeration. Of course the products from the different nations make it wonderfully interesting. Next we went to the 'Zollverein', beginning with the stuffed animals, which are really marvellous. The Zollverein room contains some very pretty objects of art: china from Munich, Berlin and Dresden, jewelry and sculpture, including 2 beautiful bronze statuettes, from Rauch's 2 Victories. We passed to the Belgian section, containing some fine furniture,—musical instruments and a beautiful marble mantlepiece etc. We only saw the one side of Austria and the Zollverein, remaining on the ground floor: so that we have still to see all that is on the opposite side and in the Galleries. The Austrian commissioner, Ritterburg, told us that the English workmen had adopted some of the Austrian tools, and theirs some of the English tools, so that both have profited. This is another result of the Exhibition, which was getting very full when we left.

May 17. Late as we were last night, we went off at ½ p. 9 to the Exhibition. We remained 2 hrs, beginning with the Spanish section, which contains very pretty things—fine black lace from Barcelona—beautiful rich brocaded stuffs from Talavera—finished blades from Toledo—most celebrated and fine collections of raw produce. The Havanna cigars made a fine show. In the same court is the Portuguese section, in which there are also fine silks, and some beautiful marbles, particularly some of a rose coloured tint, which is quite lovely, and a great deal of snuff. From here we went, still on the ground floor, to the French Court, where we remained some time, in great admiration of the room, which contains carpets and tapestry, from Aubusson and Gobelin, and the splendid specimens of Sèvres. The taste and execution are quite unequalled and gave one a wish to buy all one saw! There is every kind of porcelain, and some beautiful statues, among the latter, by Deboy, of Eve with her 2 young children, which is charming—a very pretty one of

---

[1] See Note at end of chapter.   [2] William Essex, 1784-1869.

a woman and amour by Pradier and a charming little group by Pascal. Just outside this room are fine bronzes from the antique done by that reducing machine, also a magnificent buffet, carved in wood. We next viewed the beautiful arms, clocks, fine instruments, a weighing and reducing machine for money. The remainder of the machinery we did not see. We also had visited the Italian Court—Florence, Rome and Sardinia. In the latter the Genoese velvets are quite beautiful.

May 19. At a little after 9 we went with all our guests, taking up our inspection from where we left off last time. 1st visited the North German section, but meagrely represented owing to that foolish Protectionist feeling, which will do no one but themselves harm. Hamburg has many articles in horn, some pretty furniture, a large collection of sticks, handkerchiefs, embroideries etc. Next Russia, whose department is almost entirely empty, 3rdly to America, which is certainly not very interesting, but contains some very curious inventions: small maps on gutta percha —a reaping machine etc. We crossed over and began going down the south side, which begins with America, where there was a double piano exhibited, 2 people playing at each end, which had a ludicrous effect. We then proceeded through the different German Courts, on the side of the Zollverein, including Prussia, Saxony etc. which were full of clothes of all kinds—some linen, wool, leather, bookbinding, stationery etc. Finished up with Austria, which has also clothes as well as toys, and the section of Austrian sculpture, in which there are some very pretty things by a Milanese artist, called Manti, who is living here.

May 20. Though really still feeling quite tired, got up after 8 and went immediately after breakfast, with all my guests, to the Exhibition. Our visit was entirely confined to the French section, on the south side, and we were entirely occupied in examining two Courts full of beautiful bronzes and 'orfevrerie' and pretty furniture. In the former there were bronzes of every kind and sort, plain— with gold and silver,—clocks, candelabras, ornaments etc. and of such taste, of which the beauty is beyond description, the Renaissance and Benvenuto Cellini styles being carried to the greatest perfection. In particular there was a toilette set, presented to the Dss of Parma on her marriage, by the Légitimistes. It is a perfect 'chef d'œuvre', all gold, silver and enamel, allegorical and historical figures being introduced, all executed in the most beautiful manner. In the same case was a beautiful chalice given by the Parisian clergy to the Pope—a casket given by the town of Paris to the Cte de Paris, and the sword of Gen. Cavaignac. There was also a beautiful table designed by the Duc de Luynes (who as well as M. Sallandrouze walked round with us) and some fine pieces of jewelry executed by M. Froment Meurice from whom we have bought some things. Amongst the furniture there were some clever devices, and the specimens of china inlaid in wood. We passed thro' the part where some of the French stuffs and cloths were exhibited, but as many people had come we left a little after 11.

May 21. With all our guests to the Exhibition. We saw the remainder of the French section and very agreeably, being accompanied by the Baron Ch. de Dupin and the Cte de Laborde, both on the Jury and both agreeable clever men, the former an old man, who has been Minister, the other a distinguished traveller who explained everything very well to us. We saw beautiful wood carving in furniture etc. fine bronze clocks etc., in the Nave a beautiful fountain and some statues just unpacked. Then went thro' the Courts and partitioned sections, full of shawls, most exquisite ones, Alençon lace embroidery, mantlets, embroidered shirts, bonnets, caps, gloves, the entire process of making them being shown, shoes of every sort and kind, parasols, stuffs, golden embroideries etc., also specimens of pottery, wood carving, binding, photographs, wonderful drawings or paintings for shawls etc. From France we went straight on to Turkey, the department of which is beautifully arranged, under a sort of tent, containing charming Turkish stuffs, including very fine silks, the manufacture of which was lately introduced by the Sultan into Turkey, raw materials, carpets and rugs, etc. very interesting. Got back a little before 4.

May 22 [written at Osborne, I.o.W., to which the Royal Family repaired for May 24, 'my 32nd birthday']. A very hot and heavy day. Went with our guests to the Exhibition. This time we went to the Indian Courts, visiting those on both sides, and the beautiful things in the Nave. The jewels and ornaments from Lahore are quite magnificent—such pearls—and a whole girdle of emeralds,—beautiful shawls, wood and stone carving, rude musical instruments—models of agricultural implements, and many other things, including groups of figures—fine armour etc. We then went upstairs and looked at the English china and glass, which is really beautiful, such exquisitely cut glass, with the most beautiful designs, dessert sets, bottles, wine glasses, tumblers etc. in imitation of the old Venetian glass, then such quantities of the beautiful Minton china from Staffordshire. This is upon the whole the finest. Everything for the table, bedroom sets, flower vases, all in the best taste, and many things fit to compete with the French. We then left getting back after 11. We heard that yesterday in spite of its being the day of the Derby the receipts amounted to nearly £4,000.

May 27 [back at Buckingham Palace]. Our last breakfast all together....after breakfast to the Exhibition. We 1st walked up and down the whole length of the Nave, admiring the fine statues, and all the other exhibits, then went up to the

Gallery on the other side, where are all the musical and other instruments etc., round part of the pottery. Here in the extremity of the Gallery, just above the Transept, we stopped to watch all the 1 shilling people coming in, which was a very amusing sight. They came streaming in and gazing all around. After this we went to see some beautiful artificial flowers and wax dolls etc., passing along into the foreign departments, in which we saw beautiful Brussels lace—fine instruments, carving of different kinds, from Germany, including a fine carved wood buffet and some chairs from Coburg. We passed over into the Russian section, where the things were being unpacked, and we had some glimpses of malachite.

May 29. . . . to the Exhibition. We went up to the Gallery on the south side and stood at the end of the Transept, to watch the people coming in, in streams. The sun shone very brilliantly, so much so that one had to open a parasol in the Transept. We examined all the paintings of the English and other schools, and then all the textiles—beautiful Spitalfields and other silks, shawls and stuffs from Scotland. Then next to a part in the Transept devoted to French exhibits of embroidered shawls and dresses, silks and velvets from Lyons, of all sorts and colours, really quite beautiful: one really wished one could buy a specimen of each kind. Came down again where all the light manufactures at Paris of 'barèges',[1] muslin, mousseline de soie are exhibited; the most lovely and tempting things imaginable. Made some turns round different 'countries', at which ribbons and artificial flowers were beings sold. Crossed the Nave, where there must have been 12,000—all so civil and well behaved, that it was quite a pleasure to see them.

May 30. . . . to the Exhibition. Continued just where we left off yesterday, going past the chemical productions, which are very interesting, and the crystalisation of all colours and sizes, really wonderful. Went round the straw hat manufactures and the Swiss section, where we remained some time, examining the really exquisite watches some very diminutive, barely an inch in circumference, most beautifully set with lovely enamelled exteriors of every kind and shape—one being on the top of a pencil case! The workmanship was most complicated and perfect. There was a clock which goes for a year. Passed through the Austrian and French parts, returning by the front and leaving by our usual exit. Made the acquaintance of M. Thiers, which much interested me. Should have known him at once from his prints. He was most amiable and full of praise of the Exhibition and our success, as well as of the Gov^t we possessed here.

June 1 [Windsor Castle]. Saw Grant in the garden, whom we had sent for, to come and see the Exhibition. He had never been out of Scotland.

[1] Silky dress fabric from Barèges in the Pyrenees.

June 2. After breakfast to the Exhibition. Went through all the chemical productions, preserved fruits, flowers, milk and meat of every sort;—through the beautiful collection of grain of Lawson from Scotland [*sc.* the grain collection of Lawson, a Scotch agriculturist]—saw many things made out of fibres of grass— dyed flowers—chocolate, etc. At the end of that Gallery there is a very interesting collection of guns, muskets of every sort and kind, and some very curious inventions, each of which were explained by the Exhibitors, who were all there. Some very fine swords and blades made by Wilkinson, one of which was just as pliable as a Toledo blade. We passed along behind the organ, where there were models of ships, boats, ordnance maps etc., all of which Capt. Inglefield explained to us. Went also along the other Gallery on the opposite side—through numbers of surgical instruments and appliances of every kind. When we came down and left there was a great crush but all in the best humour. There must have been at least 20,000 people at that time. Sat to Winterhalter[1] for the 1st of May picture.

June 4. Drove all round Virginia Water.

June 5. Ascot—an immense concourse of people in the best humour. We saw 5 races. The Emperor's Cup was won by 'Blacklegs' to the great grief of all the gentlemen.[2]

June 7 [back at Buckingham Palace]. To the Exhibition: went to the machinery part, where we remained 2 hours, and which is excessively interesting and instructive, and fills one with admiration for the greatness of man's mind, which can devise and carry out such wonderful inventions, contributing to the welfare and comfort of the whole world. What used to be done by hand and used to take months doing is now accomplished in a few instants by the most beautiful machinery. We saw first the cotton machines, from Oldham—the whole process of cleansing and flattening out the raw wool by which means it comes out white and soft—crushing it, combing and carding—lengthening, twisting it—and then spinning it, all in numberless machines of different kinds. We also saw the method of constructing the burring and carding machines themselves, by introducing by means of machinery little wires into pieces of cloth, thickened by rubber, forming a very elastic substance. The whole process is wonderfully neat, for the holes are bored and the wires introduced one after the other, all in a second. This is a hand machine, but all the

---

[1] F. X. Winterhalter, 1806-73, German. His full-length portrait of the Prince Consort is in the National Portrait Gallery.

[2] The Emperor's Plate was won by Mr Campbell's 'Woolwich', a last-minute substitute entry, with no money on it. Hence the nickname 'Blacklegs' (a turf swindler, wearing black gaiters) —disappointed backers of the withdrawn favourite 'giving vent to their anger in terms too strong to be mentioned' (*The Times'* report headed Thursday, 5 June).

MACHINERY COURT

others are worked by steam. There is a new invention by Mr Donisthorpe of Bradford for cleansing and combing our cotton, which is so important that he got £25,000 for selling only the 4th of the patent![1] But it would take too long to explain all the pieces of machinery we were shown. The Exhibitors were all there.

June 11. To the Exhibition, with our relatives. We went first to look at the Russian exhibits, which have just arrived and are very fine: doors, chairs, a chimney piece, a piano, as well as vases in malachite, specimens of plate and some beautifully tasteful and very lightly set jewellery.

Afterwards went to the machinery where we saw much that was most interesting, but impossible to describe in detail. The 1st part was all for making tools, and Mr Whitworth's planing of iron tools, another for shearing and punching iron of just ½ an inch thick, doing it as if it were bread!

Other machines were for making screws and rivets, another a very curious measuring machine, a knitting one, whose needles are made to move, just as if they were worked by fingers;—a packing machine, by which wool was crushed by weight, being used for compressing woollen articles etc. What was particularly interesting was a printing machine on the vertical principle, by which numbers of sheets are printed, dried and everything done in a second. We also saw some lithographic presses equally done with the greatest rapidity. We came home at ¼ to 12, and I felt quite done and exhausted, *mentally* exhausted.

June 12. After breakfast to the Exhibition. Viewed the Russian exhibits on the opposite side, among which were silk and gold brocades from Moscow, which beat the French and are really magnificent;—light silks, clothes, woollen and leather products of all kinds, grains, splendid furs, one of a black fox £3,000 in value— and a very beautiful Cashmir woven shawl, the same on both sides. We spent likewise some time in the French tapestry and Aubusson room.

June 14. . . . at the Exhibition, which it seemed quite strange to be visiting without any guests. Went 1st through one or two of the French Courts, and then upstairs, to examine in detail the Norwich shawls, of the lightest Cashmir material, also of silk, with beautiful designs, and very light Grenadine printed shawls, made in the neighbourhood of London. From here we went straight to the machinery, where we remained nearly an hour. We saw principally hydraulic machines, pumps, filtering machines of all kinds, machines for purifying sugar,—in fact, every conceivable invention. We likewise saw medals made by machinery, which not more than 15 years ago were made by hand, 50 million instead of *one* million can be

---

[1] The figure given in the *Life of Lord Masham* (S. Cunliffe Lister) who bought the patent is more modest—£2,000 for half the patent rights, and the other half later for £10,000.

supplied a week now. We concluded our visit by looking at some spinning and weaving machines. Home by ¼ to 12. Quite forgot to mention that on the morning of the 12th we saw 3 whole parishes, Crowhurst, Linchfield and Langford, from Kent and Surrey (800 in number) go by, walking in procession 2 and 2, the men in smock frocks, with their wives looking so nice. It seems that they subscribed to come to London, by the advice of the clergyman, to see the Exhibition, it only costing them 2s. and 6d.

June 16. To the Exhibition ... the whole time taken up with seeing machinery and most interesting it was. First, we saw a very curious machine for cutting wood —a curvilinear sawing machine for timber for ships, by which means it is at once cut in a curved line and tapering instead of having 1st to be sawn and then curved by manual labour;—lithographic printing in colours and varnishing;—sugar mills and sugar refiners of different kinds;—mills for grinding wheat and linseed, and for extracting oil from the latter; a machine for making biscuits. A large one, the largest in the Exhibition, invented by Mr S. Russell, for crushing sugar cane and extracting the juice, another for cleansing corn and grain;—coffee mills;—a very curious machine for making chocolate;—a very ingenious one for making cigarettes and wrapping them up in paper,—all done by the same machine—little embossing hand machines, a comb making machine; weighing ones of many different kinds; —silk spinning machines, then many models of engines, bridges, screws, one of a double propelling screw for ships, invented by Capt. Carpenter, which it is said will obviate many of the disadvantages of the screw, increasing the speed, etc. One returned feeling that in that small space, and short time, one had learnt more than one would in long journeyings.

June 17. We lunched early as Albert had to go to a meeting on the anniversary of the Society for the Propagation of the Gospel in foreign parts.

We drove out with Vicky. The park fuller of riders, walkers and carriages than I ever remember it. We heard that there had been 67,800 people, all at the same time, at the Exhibition to-day, and 65,000 yesterday! It is wonderful.

June 19. To the Exhibition. Walked entirely round the Nave, going up one way and coming down another. Then up into one of the Galleries, from which we watched the people streaming in. Uncle [*sc.* Leopold] was quite delighted with the Exhibition, saying one could *not* imagine anything more 'grandiose', or at the same time more elegant and artistic.

June 20. The 14th anniversary of my Accession. I trust I have improved since then. It seems like a dream that it should already be so long ago. We went again to the Exhibition with Uncle and his dear children. Walked round the Austrian section, the 'Zollverein' room etc., Turkey, Spain, the Sèvres room and Belgian part. . . .

June 21. A fearfully hot day—to the Exhibition going in by the great public entrance, and remaining in the corner, on the north side of that entrance. We went through the section of furs, a very fine collection, the leather, including boots and shoes, saddlery, travelling and writing cases etc., carriages, specimens of cotton of every kind and sort—quilts, cotton damask, gingham etc. with exemplifications of how the cotton is made from the pod. Mr Bazley, of the Chamber of Commerce at Manchester, explained the latter to us. Another manufacturer showed us an oriental towel, of that peculiar make of which I saw so many from Tunis, which he has made after seeing some in the making at Constantinople for *this* Exhibition. A great number of Exhibitors were there, considering the small space allotted to each. The heat was intense.

June 23. Took my first lesson in oil painting with good Winterhalter—which was successful to his and my astonishment. I find that the drawing in chalks has been of the greatest use.

Lord Aberdeen told me that the Exhibition had been the cause of everything going so smoothly in Parlt: 'I never remember anything before that *everyone* was pleased with, as is the case with this Exhibition.'

June 24. To the Exhibition and we again saw most interesting things. Went through the part with machinery, not in motion; consisting chiefly of locomotives, railway carriages of every kind and sort, constructed entirely of corrugated iron, of teak wood etc. not painted;—new modes of shifting carriages from one rail to another;—machinery for safety in case of concussion;—new sleepers and wheels of all kinds;—a machine for improving girders;—models of the 1st locomotives ever made and used in 1785, before railroads existed!: the great hydraulic lever, or press, moved by one man with which the great Tubular Bridge at Bangor was raised, which is most wonderful. We next saw models of locomotion, amongst which one of a most ingenious contrivance for transferring mail bags on railways, going at full speed, the one being caught by a machine and dropped into a sort of net, while the other is taken up. We likewise saw another very clever patent soda water machine by which soda water can be made in incredibly short time merely with gas, without any other chemical preparation. Other aerated drinks are made in the same manner. We stopped at the part where there was a collection of bibles, translated into different languages. Finished with the Indian section, with which I was very much interested. A magnificent chair, carved in ivory, sent to me by the Rajah of Travancore, is exhibited there.

June 26. With Uncle . . . to visit the Court of the Austrian sculpture, and that of the English sculpture, with which Uncle was delighted. The Gallery was very full. So was the whole building when we left, and the people so pleased to see us. It is most gratifying to see how well everyone behaves and how much they appreciate all.

June 28. This was my Coronation day; we went after breakfast to the Exhibition . . . I thought I should faint from the heat in the Gallery, where we went to look at the English jewellery and plate. Had previously been in the French Courts below, where the bronzes, jewellery and furniture are exhibited. . . . At 2 we left for Osborne. The heat in the train was fearful and made me really feel quite ill, but I was restored by the sea breeze, crossing over, as well as by the pure sweet air at Osborne.

July 1 [back at Buckingham Palace]. With Uncle and his children and Vicky to the Exhibition it being his last visit. Went through parts of the 'Zollverein' which Uncle had not yet seen. Exhibits from Belgium, guns from Hesse etc., through the Russian Court, where we examined the beautiful jewellery, things made of malachite etc., crossing over to the part where were the silks and went thro' the 'Zollverein' Courts, examining the cloth and woollen exhibits. Then we returned leaving Uncle and his sons at the Exhibition. After our luncheon Albert left me to go to Ipswich.[1]

July 5. To the Exhibition and along the Gallery in which were manufactures of animal and vegetable substances, cutlery, models and inventions of all kinds, different kinds of glass, surgical, musical etc. instruments. All the Exhibitors were summoned. I should say 100 or more, for many only exhibited *one* thing. Some of the inventions were very ingenious, many of them quite Utopian. We had rather to hurry over the electrical telegraph and other interesting instruments as Albert had a Commission waiting for him.

July 7. Albert went out early and I walked in the garden. (P.M.) . . . drove out with Albert. The Parks were immensely crowded and we met the whole Naval School, with their band, returning from the Exhibition. Many schools have visited the Exhibition, including ours from Windsor Park, each child writing a very nice account of it.

July 8. The anniversary of poor Uncle Cambridge's death. We went with the 2 girls to the Exhibition and walked down the Nave, examining the beautiful things there, in particular a new casket in ivory, come from Paris. Walked through the English furniture Courts, through those containing stoves and grates, along where the agricultural implements are, and through the machinery, where we met our agreeable instructor, Mr Hensman. He has the supervision of the whole machinery,

---

[1] To the Meeting of the British Association.

having been placed there by Mr Wm Cubitt, the Civil Engineer, an excellent clever man, cousin to *our* Cubitt, who has been most useful in the creation of the building and went round the machinery with us, explaining all so admirably and concisely. The Nave was tremendously crowded when we passed through it and the children of the Foundling Hospital were there.

July 9. We went to the Exhibition and had the electric telegraph show explained and demonstrated before us. It is the most wonderful thing, and the boy who works it does so with the greatest ease and rapidity. The alphabet is formed by marks of this sort - - - - and could easily be learnt. The number of marks implies the letters. Messages were sent out to Manchester, Edinburgh etc., the answers being received in a few seconds, truly marvellous. Col. Wylde was there to explain all to us.

We next saw the gold weighing machines used at the Bank for weighing the sovereigns and separating the light from the heavy ones. Mr Cotton, the inventor showed the machine, which is beautifully made and extremely sensitive. It has been in use for the last 9 years, and 40,000 sovereigns a day are weighed out by it! After this we went through the agricultural implements, some of which being in motion —the Exhibitors went round with us.

July 11. To the Exhibition, visiting the Italian Court and walking round the Transept, looking at all the statues round the great entrance, where all the flowers are. Then went upstairs, looked at a picture being painted of the opening and at the painted glass.

July 12 [at Windsor]. A very hot day. We went to the Exhibition—to the Gallery on the south side, going through all the exhibits of the Spitalfields silks and velvets, all the Coventry ribbons and lace from Devonshire, Nottingham, Ireland etc., as well as the plate and jewellery, the Exhibitors going round with us. It is very gratifying to see the immense improvement in taste in all the manufactures, for the greater part of which they have to thank my beloved husband. The taste of some of the plate and jewellery is beautiful; none struck us so much, as so likely to be useful for the taste of the country, as Elkington's beautiful specimens of electroplate. He had things of all kinds, imitations of the antique, of the Cinque Centi style. Mr Hope was there to show us his magnificent blue diamond. Before going into the Crystal Palace we went over the model cottage, erected by Albert just opposite. It is designed for 4 families and admirably constructed by Mr Roberts, who has built a good many other of the new lodging houses in London. We were met there by Ld Shaftesbury (Ld Ashley that was). . . .

July 13. Walked with the children in the Slopes. . . .The Terrace was crowded with people soon after luncheon, and when the bands were playing at a little after 4, the crowds were immense—many foreigners, farmers and farm labourers who had come for the Cattle Show.

July 14 [Buckingham Palace].[1] At 11 we drove down with the children to see the Cattle Show, not the Smithfield one, but the annual meeting of the Agricultural Society—for breeding stock. The Show Yard, below the Castle, looks like an encampment and is arranged in classes, under canvas, which had a very pretty effect. The animals were beautiful, and there was a very fine display of sheep and pigs—some quite as big as ponies, which, though called 'lean stock' could hardly move. But the bulls and the magnificent stallions were the most interesting. The power and strength of the Suffolk horses, all chestnuts, is extraordinary. There were also mares and foals. The Duke of Richmond and other gentlemen belonging to the Agricultural Society were there. A triumphal arch, formed of agricultural implements, had been erected close to the gate of the S. Western Railway Station.

July 15. Went to the Exhibition and looked at the glass and toys in the Austrian department on the south side and chose some of the latter for the children. Afterwards went up and walked through the Austrian silks and the Lyon silks and Parisian light stuffs, choosing some. Every day it is a new enjoyment and pleasure.

[The Queen is sitting to Landseer.][2]

July 16. Early, after lunch we went to the Exhibition. Walking up the Nave and out at the great entrance, where we examined the things that are outside: some models of roofs, anchors, specimens of coal, stone, cement etc. After that we re-entered the Crystal Palace and went to see the Indian raw produces, Dr Royle[3] meeting us and explaining to us the whole process of the making of opium, which is excessively curious. There were drawings representing the poppy fields, and the natives bleeding the poppies, which they do with a sharp instrument. Afterwards the juice that oozes out is collected and brought to the authorities to be examined by them, then it is made into curious large cakes or balls and sent to China. One of these balls was cut open for us to see and in the inside was the opium like a thick black syrup. We also saw sugar and gums of all kinds etc. The whole of the Indian section beginning with the rare products—including the splendid jewels and shawls,

[1] i.e. written at Buckingham Palace after a day spent at Windsor.

[2] Sir Edwin Henry Landseer, 1802-73. His painting of The Prince, after Shooting, with the Queen at Windsor Castle is the frontispiece in Roger Fulford's *The Prince Consort*.

[3] J. F. Royle, 1799-1858, an Indian Army surgeon. He examined the drugs sold in the bazaars in India and identified them with the medicines used by the Greeks. He recommended the introduction of cinchona plants to India (only done in 1860 after his death). A warm and active supporter of industrial exhibitions, he was one of the commissioners for the city of London in the 1851 Exhibition and was selected to superintend the Oriental Department of the Paris Exhibition of 1855.

embroideries, silver bedsteads, ivory chairs, models, is of immense interest and quite something new for the generality of people, these latter articles having hitherto only come over as presents to the Sovereign.

July 17. To the Exhibition, going 1st to see a French tile making machine, which is said to be one of the very best, also saw one or two others, and then walked through the Portuguese department, on to the Indian Court on the same side, where we chose some pretty Indian boxes for the children. Then we looked at the collection of French guns and pistols, which are beautifully made, and crossed over to the Austrian side, where we examined a very curious sort of stone or cake, possessing the ingredients of beer, and from which when dissolved good beer can be made. It is the invention of a Ct Razmowsky. Walked down to look at some French carriages etc. and at some other things 'en passant'. Again numbers of people there. Two days ago there were 74,000, of which 61,000 at once, which exceeded by 10,000 what it was considered the building could hold, and no disorder!

I took my last drive in the Park ... which I was quite sorry for, principally on account of the Exhibition, in itself so beautiful to look at—the vast crowds, the great contentment, order and loyalty, *all* have been so gratifying.

July 18 [Osborne]. Went for the last time, for the present, to the Exhibition. Went 1st to the Russian Court and there heard Erard's and Broadwood's piano played in the Nave, after which we went up into the Gallery to hear the great organ played. Examined a very curious map and globe of the moon, also several other things of interest, as we passed along. There were a great many people when we went away. Mr Dilke, Dr L. Playfair, in particular of the Commissioners, whose activity and attention are beyond all praise, as well as excellent Mr Mayne,[1] I was quite sorry to part from. Leaving London at this time of year under ordinary circumstances is a pleasure, and so it is now, the good air and quiet, but the thought grieves me that this bright time, this great epoch in our lives and in the annals of the country—this season which was looked foward to all last year with such anxiety and hope by so many, by others with trembling,—is now past. It was such a time of pleasure, of pride, of satisfaction, and of deep thankfulness, it is the triumph of peace and goodwill towards all, of art, of commerce,—of my beloved husband, and of triumph for my Country. To see this wonderful Exhibition, which has pleased *everyone* looked upon as dearest Albert's work, this has, and does indeed make me happy. The whole of this season all the Fetes, as it were, were more or less in

[1] Sir Richard Mayne, 1796-1868. Police Commissioner and promoted K.C.B., 25 October 1851. For the International Exhibition of 1862 he recruited the X division of the Metropolitan Police Force.

connection with it. The remembrance of this great undertaking and its benefit will however last for ever. The Exhibition is not to close till the end of October, and so we shall see it again.

July 20. We dined alone and spent the whole evening, sorting a number of views of the Crystal Palace, from its very first beginning, which have been published in the *Illustrated London News.*

July 31. Lord John came at 4. Talked ... of the address of the H^se of C. relative to the Crystal Palace. Ld John seemed very fair and reasonable about the latter, and we discussed the pros and cons. There were many who wished the Palace to remain for the honour of the Country and the Exhibition—others, precisely for the same reason, feared that the building might fall into decay and therefore wished it to come down,—others again, wished it to be turned into a Winter Garden. Others, and in this Ld Seymour is very much to the fore, think that the Gov^t should break faith with the public, and that for that reason it ought to come down, and a new one be built. Albert is likewise in favour of this, and we discussed all the points and different plans as to what should be done with the large surplus to perpetuate the event. It was finally agreed that an answer should be given to the address, to the effect that enquiries should be instituted into the matters of detail, before any decision could be come to.

Aug. 7 [Buckingham Palace]. Talked of our journey, of the Crystal Palace and its fate. The crossings at Hyde Park and Constitution Hill were immensely crowded with people. Otherwise London had already that look, which I think melancholy and dreary of the season being over.

Aug. 8. .... to the Exhibition and walked round the Nave and the English part, examining the beautiful things as we went along, among which there were again new ones. Our beautiful jewel case, designed by Mr Graves and executed by Elkington, stands in the Nave and is a splendid piece of workmanship. It contains our portraits in china, after Thorburn's[1] miniatures, the border, round the lower part, containing medals of the children. It is really exquisite. Every time one returns to the Exhibition, one is filled with fresh admiration of its vastness, and never tires of it and its beautiful interesting contents. One is always discovering something new. We went up into the Gallery to choose some dresses. Were greatly struck by the beautiful effect when one looks back from the Transept through the Galleries to the very end.

Aug. 9 [Osborne]. A dull heavy morning. At 9 we went to the Exhibition, going

[1] R. Thorburn of Dumfries, 1818-85, received his first commission from the Queen 1846; awarded Gold Medal, Paris 1855.

1st to look at some very curious American locks, one of which was explained to us in detail by an American. It is very extraordinary, but beyond my powers to attempt to explain. After this we looked at a small marble shrine by Mlle Megeru, and went into the 'Zollverein' room, where some new china had been placed. Viethohn was there to meet us. Visited the French bronze and jewel Court, where we were shown some new beautiful things designed by Froment Meurice, amongst which was an ivory statuette by Pradis, ornamented with turquoises etc. We walked through the Indian Court and then with quite a sad feeling bid an almost final adieu to the Exhibition, though we may still see it once or twice more just before it closes in Oct. What a glorious, unique and truly delightful work it is. What use it has been to me in so many ways, I can really hardly estimate, for it has taught me so much I never knew before—has brought me in contact with so many clever people I should never have known otherwise, and with so many manufacturers whom I would scarcely have met, unless I travelled all over the country, and visited every individual manufactory which I could never have done. At the Exhibition everything is brought together in a small space and one has all the advantage of seeing the different exhibits together. Besides, it has another, and more lasting advantage,—of gratifying all those people, whose loyalty is greatly increased by the fact of a few words being spoken to them by the highest personages—and that they will never forget. . . . Ld Wriothesley Russell . . . amused us with some very droll anecdotes of the country people who were taken to see the Exhibition. There was a killing anecdote, told us by Ld Granville, which Albert related. Someone on seeing an immense piece of alum, which is there, said 'Why, it must be Lot's wife'. Another equally good story was told of a workman, saying to another, after looking at a colossal tasteless statue of the Archangel Michael casting out Satan by M. Le Sueur 'What can it be?' When the other retorted, after some reflection 'I'll tell you what it is—that's the Queen (pointing to the angel clothed in a long robe) and that's the Pope', pointing to the grovelling fiend. A delightful idea!

Aug. 13. Albert was much occupied most of the day with the gentlemen of the Executive Committee of the Exhibition, settling alas about the closing of this great work, and considering the new great plan for the Exhibition. Mr William Cubitt remained, Albert wishing to consult him about a steam engine for our farm.

Aug. 18. At 12 we went down into the Drawing Room with all the children, ladies and gentlemen, to see a Chinese family who have just arrived, coming on purpose to see the Exhibition. . . . I annex a little sketch to give a faint idea of them. . . . The man on seeing me performed the usual very singular salutations.

Aug. 21 [at Cowes]. . . . The yachts were racing including the *America*, the new

American schooner, built upon quite a different principle to ours, and causing a great sensation at Cowes. . . . The *America* came round triumphantly, and we then set off, going slow in order to examine her. The next yacht only came round the Needles 32 minutes after her!

[*Northern Tour, August 27 to Oct. 10*: Edinburgh, Balmoral, Liverpool, Manchester —outward journey by G^t Northern, return by London and North Western —receptions at principal stations on the route.

Sept. 9. At Balmoral, 'sketched the head of Albert's stag'. *Sept. 27.* 'Mama etc. and Baron Liebig, the most distinguished Professor of Chemistry in Germany, or anywhere, dined. He is a middle aged, pleasing and quiet man. Both Beche and Dr Lyon Playfair were his pupils.'

Oct. 9. At Liverpool, 'A terribly wet day. . . . The mass of shipping is quite enormous and forests of masts are to be seen. . . . A statue of poor Sir Robert Peel is to be placed on one of the pedestals which surround the exterior of St George's Hall. To Worsley Hall, *gliding* by canal barge. . . .'

The Queen admires the drawings of Nasmyth who 'has a large factory at Patricroft, where he has a steam hammer. . . . He made the map of the moon which is in the Great Exhibition.'

Oct. 10. At Manchester, 'Fine and mild and everything à souhait.']

Oct. 12 [Windsor Castle]. Dr Lyon Playfair was with Albert talking about the Exhibition, which I cannot bear to think will be over in 3 days. The success has however been enormous: on Monday 108,000, on Tuesday 109,000, then 96,000 and again 107,000!! But they say it was dreadful on one day, when the poor old Duke of Wellington, who was visiting the Exhibition, narrowly escaped being trampled to death, there was such a rushing and squeezing, and some damage was done.

Oct. 13. After breakfast. . . to the Crystal Palace, which seemed as beautiful, bewildering and enchanting as ever, and I was delighted to find myself there again. Mr Dilke, the most indefatigable and good humoured of men, was there, as each time we have been. Walked up the Nave, towards the American part, and looked at some new things, and in the Swedish section. A piece of gold from California, and a fine vase from Sweden. Next went into the French bronze and jewels Court, admiring again all the beauty of the exhibits, and seeing some new ones by Froment-Meurice. Chose some trifles, went through the Tunisian and Turkish parts, again choosing some articles there, as I have taken from every other country. Walked through the Transept to the English side, going into the Fine Arts Court,—then

PLATE VIII

INTERIOR OF THE TRANSEPT

PLATE IX

THE EAST NAVE

PLATE X

PLATE XI

THE SCULPTURE ROOM

down the Nave to the end, through the manufactures from Manchester etc., through the part where grates, baths, iron work, lamps etc. are exhibited. Saw a very curious clock of a very peculiar mechanism. Went into the Sculpture Court, English as well as Italian etc., into the beautiful Sèvres room, which is certainly almost the finest room in the Exhibition, where we again made 'achats'. At the outside of this room is a most curious bust of a negress, pendant to the negro, which we had admired before. After this I left with the boys, Albert remaining on longer, and got back before one. . . . Forgot to mention that we had a short visit from Ld John yesterday, the chief topics of conversation being our journey, the plan of extending the suffrage and the closing of the Exhibition. We dined alone, occupying ourselves afterwards with arranging our prints of the Exhibition, from illustrated papers, which make a very beautiful collection, from the very first construction of the building with all its details and views of every kind, as well as newspaper articles.

Oct. 14. After breakfast started for the Exhibition. . . . It looked so beautiful and I could not believe that it was the last time I should behold this wonderful creation of my beloved Albert's. An organ accompanied by a fine and powerful instrument called the sarrusophone[1] was being played. We walked through the French machinery, and then up to the Gallery along the front one, and all the way round. The view from near the end, close to the last entrance, one can never carry in one's mind—each time one is amazed afresh at the immense length and height and the fairy like effect of the different objects that fill it. Walked in fact through the whole building, bidding it regretfully adieu. Preparations were already being made for to-morrow's closing ceremony. An old Cornish woman, wearing a very singular hat—aged 80, who walked up several 100 miles to see the Exhibition, was at the door to see us, a most hale old woman who was almost crying from emotion, when I looked at her. We were back at Windsor by ½ p. 12.

Oct. 15. This dear day is the 12th anniversary of our engagement! A very wet day. At 10 Albert started for the ceremony of the Closing of the Exhibition, which was not to be in state. I grieved not to be able to be present, and yet I think Albert was right, that I could hardly have been there as a spectator.—Writing and reading etc. Albert was back by 2. All had gone off well. Everyone seemed pleased. The crowds immense, he thinks from 40 to 50,000 people—closely packed. Albert on the beautiful Indian chair, presented by the Rajah of Travancore, at the head of a table round which sat the Commissioners, all on a platform, read a long answer to Ld Canning, who, as Chairman of the Committee of Jurors, had read a detailed report. A prayer was offered by the Bishop of London, followed by the singing of

---

[1] Named after the French inventor Sarrus, and patented 1856.

the Hallelujah, the whole proceedings having begun with 'God save the Queen': Albert was *most* enthusiastically received. It unfortunately rained a little. Messrs Dilke, Paxton (for whom this is indeed an immense, though deserved distinction, and very striking as to the possibility of the lowest being able, by their own merits, to rise to the highest grade of society,—he was only a gardener's boy), Mr Cubitt, and Mr Fox are to be knighted; Dr Lyon Playfair, Mr Cole and Sir Stafford Northcote to be Companions of the Bath, and Col. Reid and Mr Mayne (already Companions) Commanders of the Bath. To think that this great and bright time is past, like a dream, after all its success and triumph, and that all the labour and anxiety it caused for nearly 2 years should likewise now be only remembered as 'a has been' seems incredible and melancholy.

Oct. 19. I here copy part of a letter from Ld John Russell, in which he expresses himself very properly about the Exhibition. 'The sad solemnity of the closing of the Exhibition was as successful as it was possible to be. In taking leave of it there is one result which must be particularly gratifying to Y^r Majesty. The grandeur of the conception, the zeal, invention and talent displayed in the execution, and the perfect order maintained from the first day to the last have contributed to give imperishable fame to P^{ce} Albert. If to the others much praise is due, for their several parts in this work,—it is to his energy and judgment that the world owes both the original design and the harmonious and rapid execution. Whatever may be done hereafter, no one can deprive the Prince of the glory of being the first to conceive and carry into effect this beneficent design. Nor will the monarchy fail to participate in the advantage to be derived from this undertaking. No Republic of the Old or New World has done anything so splendid or so useful.' This is very true. Albert has written most kind autograph letters to Ld Granville, Col. Reid, Mr Cubitt, Mr Cole, Mr Dilke and Dr Lyon Playfair. He gives them and others commemoration medals. I have sent Mrs Dilke a bracelet, as she was so very assiduous in executing all our commissions. I have also sent souvenirs to Mr Dilke, Dr Lyon Playfair and Mr Cole.—We dined alone, and went to the Print Room, and played duets.

Oct. 23. At 1 had audiences. First knighted . . . Mr Paxton, Mr Cubitt and Mr Fox, all of whom seemed quite 'emu' and excessively happy.

A Council, after which we received Mr J. Shepherd and Sir James Weir Hogg, Deputy Chairman of the East India Company. These had been deputed by the E. Indian Directorate to present me with 'a specimen of each of the principal articles exhibited by the East India Company, in grateful recollection of the patronage vouchsafed by me 'to the Great Exhibition of the Works of All Nations and in particular to the Indian Section'. I annex[1] a list of the beautiful and interesting things 'offered for my acceptance', which are of immense value and most curious and tasteful. The jewels are truly magnificent. They had also belonged to Runjat Singh and been found in the Treasury at Lahore. The very large pearls, 224 in number, strung in 4 rows, are quite splendid and a very beautiful ornament. The girdle of 19 emeralds is wonderful and also of immense value. The emeralds, square in shape and very large, are alternately engraved, and unfortunately all are cut flat. They are set round with diamonds, and fringed with pearls. The rubies are even more wonderful, they are cabochons, unset but pierced. The one is the largest in the world, therefore even more remarkable than the Koh-i-noor! I am very happy that the British Crown will possess these jewels, for I shall certainly make them Crown Jewels.

Nov. 11. To Buckingham Palace, where we gave some directions relative to the numerous things we have bought at the Exhibition, and also things that have been given. Then we went to the Crystal Palace. The flags have been removed and the English side is almost entirely empty. On the foreign side, there are still a good many things left, but not many in the Galleries, and everywhere there are numerous packing cases. The organ is left. The canvas is entirely removed, and the beauty of the building, with the sun shining through, was never seen to greater advantage. One cannot bear to think of its all coming down, and yet I fear it will be the best and wisest thing. Mr Dilke, Sir R. Mayne and Mr Cole were there—It is sad to think all is past now!

[1] The list, which is bound into the Diary, runs to several pages. It includes silver filigree of Cuttack and Travancore, Persian seals carved at Delhi, Cashmere shawls worked in gold and pearls, muslins of Dacca, Benares scarves of gold blended with different colours. Tussore silks, carpets, rugs and velvets, sandal wood, ivory carvings, temple models, gongs, agate cups of Cambay, a porcupine quill basket, mats from Malabar, and the True Spikenard of the Ancients from the Himalayas.

NOTES

The position with regard to photography in 1851 was as follows: The Queen refers to Daguerreotypes and photographs, which correctly separates the achievements of that date. There was the Daguerreotype itself, patented in 1839, which was a direct photograph made upon the metal plate—at first reversed and later corrected with a prism. This photograph was rendered positive and always enclosed in a glass case to prevent the rubbing of the surface which completely ruins it. The Daguerreotype was at a high level of craftsmanship by 1851, and there are many beautifully hand-tinted examples, as well as the ordinary kind.

The other kind of photography was Fox-Talbot's Calotypes—also patented in 1839—which were photographs in the modern sense of the word in that the negative was made, as to-day, on paper instead of glass or celluloid, and the prints produced, again as to-day, by printing through this thin paper negative on to another piece of prepared paper. It was these that were referred to as 'photographs' by the Queen. (It is unlikely that the new invention of the wet-plate by Scott Archer, 1851, was shown to her, in the absence of comment to that effect.) The two types of photography may be distinguished thus: the Daguerreotype was pin-sharp and with wonderfully fine detail, but could never be reproduced, as each one was unique. Very many Daguerreotypes of the Exhibition were taken, but next to none have survived.

The Calotype gained in breadth and type of treatment what it lost in detail; and although they were used for detailed subjects, their beauty and value depended more on their softness and pictorial qualities. The Jury Reports of the Great Exhibition, in the specially bound edition, were illustrated with these Calotypes. (Cf. Huxley to his sister, 6 May 1846, from the *Rattle-snake*: 'I have learnt the calotype process for the express purpose of managing the Calotype apparatus, for which Captain Stanley has applied to the Government'—L. Huxley, *Life and Letters of T. H. Huxley*, I, 39.)

Such was the beginning of an art destined to play a great role alike in peace and war. It is of interest that in 1853 instruction in photography was being given at Gore House on the South Kensington estate to sappers and engineers for Ordnance purposes.

See the admirable account of W. H. Fox-Talbot and Lacock Abbey in the *Illustrated London News* of 11 February 1950.

In the documents, till towards the end, Prince Albert is the Prince or H.R.H. Prince Albert, not the Prince Consort; and a letter from the Queen to the King of the Belgians explains the position. 'I wish to tell you of a step which is to be taken, and which will, I am sure, meet with your concurrence. You know the people call Albert "Prince Consort", but it never had been given him as a title, so I intend to confer it on him merely by Letters Patent, just as I conferred the precedence on him in 1840—I should have preferred its being done by Act of Parliament, and so it may still be at some future period: but it was thought better on the whole to do it *now* by this simple way.'

This was done on 25 June 1857. There was no subsequent Act of Parliament.

CHAPTER V

THE EXHIBITS

THERE were Britons who did not share Queen Victoria's sentiments of pride and frank admiration. Dickens, for instance, wrote:

I find I am 'used up' by the Exhibition. I don't say there is nothing in it—there's too much. I have only been twice; so many things bewildered me. I have a natural horror of sights, and the fusion of the many sights in one has not decreased it. I am not sure that I have seen anything but the fountain and perhaps the Amazon. It is a dreadful thing to be obliged to be false, but when anyone says, 'Have you seen....?' I say, 'Yes', because if I don't, I know he'll explain it, and I can't bear that!![1]

But those who expressed (and no doubt even the greater number who shared) Dickens's views were in a minority. For the whole period of the Exhibition the public streamed in. The attendance figures are indeed impressive.

The official returns worked out as follows:

The Exhibition was open from 1 May to 15 October 1851, Sundays and the final Monday and Tuesday excluded, and in that time, 140 days, there were 6,063,986 visitors. This included many who paid more than one visit. The season ticket-holders, c.25,000, made nearly 800,000 visits, and there were c.17,000 exhibitors attending daily in the course of business; how many of these were ticket-holders is not known. No means of assessing the overlap here, or of calculating multiple visits by genuine visitors, appear to exist, but at a guess four million persons must have paid one or more visits. This would be considerably more than the number of the whole population of Greater London at the time: and if we allow half a million for foreign and Irish

---

[1] Walter Dexter, *Letters of Charles Dickens*, vol. II, p. 327, Dickens to the Hon. Mrs Richard Watson, from Broadstairs, Kent, 11 July 1851.

visitors, then something like 17 per cent of the total population of Great Britain, men, women and children, actually saw the Exhibition.

Financially, it was the shilling visitors, 4,440,000 of them, who ensured success, for they paid at the doors £220,000 out of the total takings of

SHILLING DAY

£357,000. Monday to Thursday were shilling days; Fridays, half-crown, and Saturdays, five shillings (after 2 August, half-crown). Half-crown visitors paid £77,000 and five-shilling visitors £61,000. The two days after the opening day were £1 days, but the takings were only £1,042. Adding to the £357,000 taken at the doors the £68,000 paid for season tickets, we have as the total of entrance money, £425,000—a respectable sum, which in terms of 1951 values should be multiplied by four at least. Comparisons of the changing value of money are dangerous ground, but it is apposite to record that the 1,800 (mostly skilled) workmen who erected the structure averaged 28s. a week in wages. What will they be earning on the similar job to-day?

PLATE XII

A. THE SHILLING DAY—GOING TO THE EXHIBITION

B. THE SHILLING DAY—EXTERIOR OF THE EXHIBITION

PLATE XIII

A. AGRICULTURISTS AT THE EXHIBITION

B. THE FIVE-SHILLING DAY

PLATE XIV

CANADIAN EXHIBITS

PLATE XV

A. THE RIVER

B. HYDE PARK

The attendances, always greatest on one-shilling days, increased to a first peak of 68,000 on Wednesday, 17 June, then declined; but on 15 July, they were up to a new peak of 74,000; there was then a steady decline through August to a 'low' of 38,000 on 27 August. It must have been unbearably hot in that mammoth glasshouse in August, especially when it is considered what masses of clothes they wore in those days. In September the public came back, and by the 30th the attendance was up to 69,000 again. But the last week of the Exhibition provided a statistical thrill for the Commissioners, for on three days these last-moment visitors exceeded 100,000, the peak figure being 109,915 on Tuesday, 7 October.

The Commissioners in their 1852 Report take 6,039,195 as their total of visits, and put the average daily takings on a 140-day basis at £2,548. The average of the first three weeks was £2,546: and from this they conclude with satisfaction (1) that the scale of charges was so apportioned as to place all classes on an equal footing; (2) that the reduction of rates came at the very time which experience showed to be the one best adapted for ensuring the financial success of the undertaking (*1852 Report*, p. 53).

How will it work out in 1951? At the British Empire Wembley Exhibition of 1924 there were 17,403,267 visitors; which on similar assumptions to those made above means that 23 per cent of the population of Great Britain visited it. Considering the development of transport facilities between 1851 and 1924, and the special Wembley attractions of military tattoos, etc., the performance of 1851 was remarkable, and there can be no doubt that its impact on the imagination was greater by far.

In their moments of leisure these crowds were permitted neither to smoke nor to drink—a fact hailed, as the *Daily News* reports on 6 August 1851, by a mass parade of 15,000 teetotallers who, in the intervals of demonstrating, refreshed themselves *con amore* at the transept fountain. But non-alcoholic refreshments were available. Schweppe's were the contractors for the Refreshment Court, taking £45,000 with Bath buns, plain buns, soda water, lemonade and ginger beer as leaders. A plate of ham was available for 6d. at the refreshment rooms, bread and butter for 2d., Schweppe's Soda Water for 6d., ices for *6d.* and *1s.*—the ices being frozen in a patent machine by the aid of steam, as shown in the Exhibition.

The intake of food and drink was not, however, the proudest achievement of 1851: here were the first public conveniences, some free, some not. (Receipts from the latter were £2,441, profit £1,769.) So impressed was the Royal Society of Arts by this triumph of money over nature, that it endeavoured after the Exhibition to introduce them to the streets of London. This time the conveniences did not pay, and they had to await the time when they should rank as a public service, as they did under the subsequent direction of Sir William Haywood, the City engineer, who made central London the most convenient capital in Europe.

Visitors came to the Exhibition from far and wide. The Great Exhibition, indeed, saw the birth of the modern excursion train. Lord Willoughby d'Eresby was reported to have hired a town house for his tenants visiting it. Five hundred people came from Harlow, Cambridgeshire, in a special train, single fare for double journey, then to Hyde Park in vans, *6d.* a head. On one day (16 June) twenty excursions pulled into Euston. The fare: *20s.* from Liverpool, *18s. 6d.* from York—with stop-over for a few days. Many firms sent their men, many schools were later to send their pupils. Philip Pusey brought 500 of his labourers to the Exhibition on Midsummer Day, 1851, and received in return a presentation silver snuff-box in memory of this visit. In almost every cottage in Pusey (near Faringdon, Berks) there is an engraving with his portrait and autograph and a representation of the snuff-box beneath.

Visitors, too, came from abroad. Charles Dickens's *Household Words* hailed this invasion:

I am of opinion that the editors of foreign newspapers will no longer declare that we live on raw beef-steaks, and occasionally eat the winners of our Derbies; that every nobleman takes his 'bouledogue' to court with him; that we are in the daily habit of selling our wives in Smithfield market; and that during the month of November three-fourths of the population of London commit suicide. Altogether I think that a little peace, and a little good-will, and a little brotherhood among nations will result from the foreign invasion; and that it will in future no longer be a matter of course that because 50,000 Frenchmen in blue coats and red trousers meet

50,000 Englishmen in blue trousers and red coats, they must all fall to and cut or blow each other to atoms.[1]

Behind the organized tours and excursions came private visitors of all classes. A visit to the Crystal Palace was so great an experience that it was worth a considerable effort. Witness, for instance, the workman whose feat of endurance the *Daily News* reported with admiration. He left Huddersfield on the night of 22 July for London, with only a few sandwiches in his pocket and a shilling in his purse, after paying his fare of 5s. for a third-class railway ticket. He paid his shilling to see the Exhibition in the Crystal Palace. He ate his sandwiches in the building and drank from the crystal fountain, returned home the next night and resumed his work on the Thursday morning without having spent a farthing for either lodgings, eating or drinking during the forty hours he was from home.

Others came by bus: a proceeding not without its emotional strains. Thus the *Daily News* (14 July 1851) complained bitterly of 'the increasing exactions and insolent conduct of the omnibus people. On wet days they absolutely run riot, refusing passengers for less than a shilling fare, and those which are appointed to run to long distances, such as Kennington and Islington, actually declining passengers for those distances at any price, in order that they may make short journeys to Charing Cross for which they insist on the full fare. The insolence of the conductors on these occasions is unbearable. They slam the door in any passenger's face who disputes their exactions and tell them to summon him.' On the other hand the paper handsomely acknowledged that drivers worked seventeen hours a day in all weathers. Since the season had been incredibly profitable to their proprietors, why, it asked (13 September 1851), did the latter not send them to the Exhibition?

Let us, therefore, join the crowds and make our own tour of the Great Exhibition with its 15,000 exhibitors. The Crystal Palace housed the inventions of others.

Once inside it we shall be so mazed with their variety, not to speak of the

---

[1] On the other hand *Punch*, taking it for granted that the Tories did the wrong thing, drew an old Tory hanging out a bill: 'Ici on ne parle pas français'—to keep foreigners away.

palms and the statuary and the crowd itself, that we shall find it hard to organize our thoughts. Let us try, therefore, to think it out in advance. What sort of reply could the England of 1851 make to the rest of the world in the industrial field?

The first half of the nineteenth century teemed with textile inventions, the great majority being small improvements on the master ideas of the eighteenth century. The key invention of the nineteenth century was the wool-combing machine, in which after many years of experiment England took the lead with the patents of Lister, Holden and Noble, 1851-3 (though in its way the machine comb of the Alsatian, J. Heilmann, was as good). This improvement in the preparation of the fabric was accompanied at the finishing end, notably in knitting and lace-making, by improved machines for producing elaborate patterns by power. The 1840's saw the circular knitting machine (a French invention in the first instance) and Livesay's (Nottingham) lace-curtain machine; and both in hosiery and lace British invention was predominant. In textile alternatives, too, Britain was to the fore—with silk waste for silk, jute for flax, worsted pile for velvet. And the by-product (e.g. Mungo and Shoddy) was slowly coming into its own.

Our strength in hosiery is seen in the story of the firm of Hollins, 1784-1949, written by Stanley Pigott for William Hollins and Co. Ltd., Viyella House, Nottingham.

In the 1851 Exhibition, this firm's exhibit (Manufactures No. 30) was thus described: 'Hollins, Williams & Co., Pleaseley Works near Mansfield, Nottingham, manufacturers, merino, cashmere and cotton hosiery yarns, used in the Midland counties for the manufacture of hosiery, and on the Continent for knitting and hosiery purposes.'

The important word is 'merino'. Notts spinners had mastered cotton (the earliest cotton factory was in this county), but to provide good hosiery yarn from long-fibred wool was technically difficult. To overcome this difficulty, with the firm of Hollins leading the way, 'they seized upon the particular feature of the Australian supply; for merino wool, excellent in quality, is short in fibre and thus it was found to blend extremely well with cotton.

The two could be spun together into a single mixed yarn which possessed the failings of neither material and the virtues of both.' Later in its career, the same firm, bringing back ideas from the Paris Exhibition of 1889, introduced its famous *Viyella* cloth. *Viyella* comes from *Via Gellia*, the fanciful name of a road outside Crompton in Derbyshire, on which the Via Gellia Spinning Co., acquired by Hollins, was located.

In the iron and steel industry the master idea was the Bessemer Converter of 1856, with its complement, the Siemens Open Hearth. These provided a new material for shipbuilding, engineering, and tall structures, but as steel, though technically distinct, is in appearance like iron, there was nothing very novel to put on show. The novelty was the process, which could not be shown in an exhibition ground. What could be shown was electro-plate, the patent for which Siemens sold to Elkington in 1842.[1] The age of steel was the the age also of industrial chemistry. John Mercer of Accrington, Lancs, gave his name to mercerized cotton. In 1846 paper was being made by the caustic soda process. By 1854 aluminium was being obtained in considerable quantities by the castner sodium process. In 1856 Sir William Perkin discovered the first aniline dye. In 1857 James Clerk Maxwell, the mathematical physicist, synthesized white light from red, green and blue rays (incidentally, the carpet-makers of Persia and India had for centuries dyed by the three-colour process). During the 1850's Lawes and Gilbert at Rothamsted were testing the values of artificial fertilizers. The parent brain in the agricultural field was Liebig; and in chemistry generally Germany was level with, and in some departments ahead of, England. The mid-century witnessed also the arrival of vulcanized rubber, ebonite, artificial refrigeration and the sewing-machine. Here America led the way, as also in numerous labour-saving devices called for in a country where resources were enormous and manpower short.

But invention is a continuous stream, and I do not suggest that the mid-century was more epochal than 1825 on the one side, with its steam railway, and 1875 on the other, when Graham Bell at Brantford, Ontario, mastered the secret of the telephone, and Gilchrist Thomas discovered how to eliminate

---

[1] Electro-plate is a very thin layer of silver deposited by electrolysis on a less noble metal.

phosphorus from pig-iron. The significance of 1851 was rather that machinery was in the ascendant, and handicraft at the same time so rich that its general eclipse was not in sight. Like the ship of sail and wood, it was under challenge, but never so impressive as in its latter days. The commixture of old and new, with the old swollen by the art treasures of Europe and the East, gave to the Great Exhibition its peculiar interest. But a great show fails in its purpose if it is not accessible to the multitude. There is therefore a further significance in the fact that by 1851 the main lines of the British railway system were in operation to London.

Bearing such facts in mind let us look at the British contributions to the Exhibition, following the path already trodden by Mr Christopher Hobhouse in his *1851 and the Crystal Palace*.[1]

The layout of the Exhibition—Henry Cole was responsible for it—was as follows:

(i) Foreign and colonial goods in the east half of the building, the countries nearest to the Equator being nearest to the transept.

(ii) British goods in the west half, the lighter articles in the galleries.

(iii) Machinery on the north, adjacent to the steam-pipes by which they were set in motion; manufactures and fine arts spaced intermediately, each having some share of the frontage on the central avenue.

BRITISH CONTRIBUTIONS

At the approach, a colossal statue of Richard Cœur de Lion, which remained at Sydenham to the end: and a second monster, a block of 24 tons of coal from the Duke of Devonshire's Stavely mines near Chatsworth. (Symbols of Courage and Power!)

We enter the building to see the largest sheet of plate-glass ever made and a miscellany of mineral ores and foodstuffs; also a model of the Liverpool Docks (Britain the great metropolitan consumer). Machinery, headed by locomotives and other railway equipment: James Watt of Soho: the hydraulic press which lifted the Britannia tubular bridge: Mr Shillibeer's expanding

[1] London, 1937 (New Edition, 1950)

hearse. Manufacturing machines and tools—James Nasmyth's steam-hammer easily first, being so big and so gentle. Bridges and lighthouses. Ship models and lifebelts. A prodigious assemblage of sporting arms, but 'so far as possible the Commissioners had excluded weapons of aggression from the Temple of Universal Peace'. Agricultural implements, drawing a rural crowd, which to Mr Hobhouse is more attractive than the implements themselves. Among philosophic instruments the great Ross telescope and some photographic apparatus; balloons of course, for it was the age of balloon flights, and musical instruments galore. Pianos by Broadwood, Collard, etc. Clocks and watches and surgical instruments, which strove to outdo one another in fantasy. 'One exhibitor offered a physician's walking stick which contained an enema and some test-tubes.'

Here inevitably the textiles took first place. England had made its money in cotton, though it was now eagerly investing it in railways. There were fabrics, and clothing made from them. After that came boots and shoes made of leather, which introduces us to skins and furs and the exhibits of the Hudson's Bay Company. The hardware displayed was a real miscellany—grates and a gas cooker, cast-iron railings and the locks and safes of Chubb and Milner.

Next come precious metals and jewellery. Here Mr Hobhouse, whose main interests are artistic and not economic, is a lively guide. When the testimonial plate of the age is on view, Puck threatens to run away with his pen, though even here he keeps a sense of proportion. The standard of to-day, he thinks, is lower than that of 1851, and 'the candelabra were really lovely'.[1] But we are waiting to be told about the Koh-i-noor, and Mr Hobhouse tells it well, allowing himself one of his very few notes, the text and note reading:

The Koh-i-noor, lately acquired by the East India Company with the rest of the contents of the Treasury of Lahore, and by them presented to the Queen, was shown in a large gold bird-cage in the east nave. Its weight was then 186 carats, but it was still in its crude form, an ungainly lump of stone. A subsequent recutting in Amsterdam has given it its brilliance, but reduced its weight to 106 carats.

[1] See Plate 4, p. 37, in Cruikshank's *Charles Dickens and Early Victorian England*.

Note: Some foreigners formed a plot to steal the Koh-i-noor. One of them, a woman, was to faint immediately in front of it, and the others were to rush to her assistance. It was given away by a servant at their lodgings. The cage was made by Chubb's and the jewel was lowered into its massive pedestal at night.[1]

We are now at glass, and again the wanted information is forthcoming:

The glass section was small, but the standard high. The industry had only come to life since the removal of the excise duty in 1845; Chance Brothers, the contractors of the glass for the Crystal Palace, were the only large makers, and they relied for much of their work on foreign labour.

Then comes pottery and furniture, Wedgwood exhibiting his famous copy of the Portland Vase, and Pugin, daringly, in his Medieval Court, the ornaments of ritualism. A Fine Arts Commissioner for the Exhibition, Pugin died within a year of its close. 'Protestant architects took over the benefit of his researches and propaganda, but there was no one to capture his inspiration.'

Finally sculpture (painting being excluded by the regulations)—'sculpture by the ton, but not one single piece of good sculpture'; at this, therefore, let us leave it, with the foreknowledge that that from the Continent was much better.

Inevitably it is the machinery exhibited in the Crystal Palace that interests us most, as it did the contemporary visitor. This had not been anticipated. 'Machinery, we fear, will not form the most popular, however it may be the most extensive department of the Exhibition.' The reporter of the *Daily News* was mistaken, as northern visitors thronged in to see it, topping the 100,000 mark in the last hectic week. He was, however, right in laying stress on the engineering exhibits. 'There is a most excellent show of manufacturers' machines and tools. Sharp has a good collection, so has Hick—but Whitworth's seems the best.'

Machinery was in two sections, moving machinery and machinery at rest. Whitworth's stand of engine-tools—Appold's centrifugal pump—four-cylindered marine engines—the great hydraulic press from the Britannia Bridge; but of such enumeration there would be no end. Cannot we view them

[1] Pp. 102-3.

in large, and classify? Dr Lyon Playfair essayed it: and this was his subdivision:

1. Machines for direct use.
2. Manufacturing machines and tools.
3. Mechanical, civil engineering and architectural contrivances.
4. Naval architecture and military engineering.
5. Agricultural and horticultural machines and implements.
6. Philosophical, musical, horological, acoustic and miscellaneous.

'Miscellaneous' is not very logical, but according to the author it worked. He and the French Commissioner had an argument on the subject:

My French colleague had a handsome walking-stick in his hand, and proposed that this should be the test. Turning to my class of 'Miscellaneous objects', under the subsection 'Objects for Personal use', I readily found a walking-stick. The French Commissioner searched his logical classification for a long time in vain, but ultimately found the familiar object under a subsection 'Machines for the propagation of direct motion'. He laughed heartily, and agreed to work under the English classification.[1]

Then come minerals—coal, iron, stone, copper, lead, etc., the smaller specimens being inside the building, and in particular the collection from the mines at Allenhead in Northumberland.

We, with A. Raistrick's *Two Centuries of Industrial Welfare (The London Quaker Lead Co.), 1692-1905,* before us, know the fascinating story of which this collection was a visible sign. But we are very tired, and it is so hot within the building that we are glad to know there is one last exhibit which can be viewed only in the open air:

Large masses of coal and cement and concrete, and several examples of the Welsh, Cornish, Scotch and Irish slates and flags, were exhibited on the south side; while on the north, were several atmospheric apparatuses for recording meteorological observations, admiralty anchors, and granite columns and obelisks.

There lies the fuel of industry, which makes the whole thing go. Our strength is on the seas: look at the girth of those anchors, which even the Cape Breton

---

[1] Wemyss Reid, *Memoirs . . . of Lyon Playfair,* p. 116.

giant could not have heaved overboard. We shall one day conquer the air, having begun abroad in 1851 to observe its behaviour. But to-day and every day the machines will run on, provided that there is fuel to feed them. They could stop, but they must not. Heaven help the cement if it hardens!

We have already inspected the imperial and colonial exhibits in the company of the Queen. Let us only note here that seven whole sections were devoted to them.

Do we not see how nonsensical it is to talk of the 'Little Englandism' of the 1850's and 1860's? It was anything but this—call it insular megalomania, if you will, to suppose that an island without a preferential tariff could focus on itself the trade of its colonies and overseas possessions without losing their allegiance. It was because Britain believed she had things to offer to them as to the rest of the world, which whether the world wanted them or not was destined to enter into its consumption, that she bestrode with such nonchalance the free-trade horse. For she was herself the supply side of the Industrial Revolution.

Note next the territorial dispersion of the Empire. West Indies, colonies, etc: 'colonies etc.' embracing Australia and New Zealand! From the West Indies come specimens of sugar by Mr H. Warner (a great West-Indian name); of pitch from the Pitch Lake of Trinidad; of tropical flowers, vegetable products and fruits modelled in wax. Guernsey and Jersey, Malta and Ceylon a comical commixture, but they were entrepôt islands on the way to Europe and the East, significant alike in war and peace. And then there was India whence came the Koh-i-noor and other treasures, such as the gold-mounted saddle, set with jewels, of the late Ranjit Singh. (He had been the ruler of the Sikh kingdom and in his defeat contributed more to the Exhibition than any other personage!)

Canada by sheer simplicity achieved one of the pictorial successes of the Exhibition—moose and elk, birch-bark canoes and sleighs, and the first demonstration of the mineral wealth which is the supreme asset of Canada to-day. In the middle ground was a machine testifying to Canada's age-long fight against forest fire. 'The first engine was very ingeniously constructed and could throw a jet of water to a height of 180 feet, only requiring twenty to thirty men to work.'

Lastly, 'as an illustration of the beauty and aptness of the native woods for cabinet work, there were six chairs, elaborately carved in the style of the fourteenth century, the coverings of which were worked by the ladies of Montreal, sent over and exhibited previous to being presented to Her Majesty'. They must have started work on it very shortly after their gentlemen had advocated annexation to the United States!

What had foreign countries to show against this impressive display? With courteous showmanship, the foreign display came first. Exhibits from Greece to America thus spanned in space and time the economic civilization of the West.[1]

In 1851 the GREECE of Pericles and the Elgin marbles was represented by some parcels of currants and several minor works of art; but the Elgin marbles are in the British Museum and the heritage of Greece is in our minds—its philosophy, its literature, its art. This puts economics in its place.

RUSSIA was late in 1851, owing to frozen waters, but towards the close came along with a rush. There was malachite from the mineral wealth of Russia which one day, behind its iron curtain, will explode the atom bomb, but which in 1851 testified to the love of the Russian court for gorgeous ornament, fashioned by western craft.

NORTH GERMANY. The exhibits are so few that we have time for something more important, the evolution of the German Zollverein. Where had Germany got to in 1851? By 1834 the Prussian Customs Union, composed at the outset of two areas, Prussia proper and Prussian Rhineland, was integrated by the adhesion of the Middle German Trade Union, comprising Saxony and the Thüringen States. By 1851 the integration had proceeded further, but Hanover, Schleswig-Holstein and Mecklenburg, together with Hamburg and

---

[1] The authorities had solved the technical problems posed by the mass of foreign goods very neatly. The Palace was in fact a great bonded warehouse. There was a regular Customs establishment within the building, consisting of a surveyor and subordinate officers, and these passed the goods free of duty to the exhibitors on the understanding that the contents of the invoice would be forthcoming at the close of the Exhibition or else duty paid by the proprietors.

other Hanse towns, were still outside it, as also was Austria. There was thus in Germany a conflict of fiscal freedoms. Those outside the Prussian scheme wished to avoid absorption by Prussia, and English diplomatists supported them, seeking by trade reciprocity to assure British trade an entry into German markets. Those inside the Prussian scheme desired to intensify and extend the area of effective Free Trade; and this school prevailed. The Prince and Princess of Prussia were the most honoured guests at the Exhibition: their son, whom they brought with them, was to marry one day the Princess Royal of England; and it is permissible to think that the support thus given by the British royal family to the cause of a greater Germany inclined British statesmen to ally their country, by way of compensation, with the Emperor Napoleon in Turkey and the Crimea. At any rate, the Zollverein responded liberally to the invitation to partake in the Exhibition.

HOLLAND is outside the sweep of the Industrial Revolution, for she had no coal. But Amsterdam was famous as a cutter of diamonds, and she sent enough of her rare products and 'philosophic instruments' to remind the world of her commercial and cultural standing.

BELGIUM is as emphatically inside its sweep—500 exhibitors from the little kingdom of Uncle Leopold, which already was adept in the exhibition art from national displays held in turn in Brussels, Antwerp and Ghent. With only two kings, Leopold I and Leopold II, in the 78 years from 1831 to 1909 she was dynastically as stable as England, and because no one was jealous of him, the second Leopold was allowed to acquire an African empire in the Congo. The Empress of India, perhaps, smiled at the audacity, but Belgium is still in the Congo, and in India where are we?

AUSTRIA. Here is real taste alike in manufacture and fine art—taste, more-over, which was clinched by personal feeling and the sense of smell. For the brain is mazed by countless names, and the eye blinded by countless objects. But behold the Gothic book-case, carved in oak, presented to the Queen by the Emperor of Austria, and smell at the eau-de-Cologne fountain. 'This delicious perfume was so liberally distributed, that the supply in charge of the attendant was exhausted before the Jury had made their awards, so that a further supply had to be obtained from a cask in the custody of H.M.'s Customs.' You remember a smell when you have forgotten an object or a fact.

The Zollverein has upwards of 1700 exhibitors, nearly equalling in number those from France. Didactic objects are prominent, like the silver fruit-dish which represented the gradual attainment of civilization by mankind. Albert, too, was a German, and one thinks of the ornamentation of the Albert Memorial. But—the Octagonal Room has specimens of wood carving, bronzes and statuary from the best things in the galleries of Munich, Dresden and Berlin.

FRANCE had not one court, but five, with Lyons silk, Sèvres porcelain, Gobelin tapestry, Aubusson carpets; and in the work of her goldsmiths and silversmiths the emphasis was less on the weight of metal than on the perfection of workmanship and design. France, we say, never had an industrial revolution: only in her politics did she break violently from her past. State enterprise, and taste in conjunction with manual skill, come through, unbroken, to the present. It is probably true that if France had boycotted the Exhibition, it would have been a failure. Great, therefore, was the service of Cobden's friend, Michael Chevalier, in scotching the project of French protectionists for a rival 'international' in this same year.

SPAIN and PORTUGAL, shadows of their old imperial selves, sent raw produce such as merino wool, and could have sent wines; Toledo ware also, from the Royal Ordnance of Toledo, and snuffs from the Royal Tobacco Contractors of Lisbon. For these last the Jury awarded an honourable mention, but 'the Company, by their liberality, constituted all the visitors to the Crystal Palace jurors, and were able to judge the high appreciation which the latter evinced for the quality of the tobacco, by the rapid manner in which whole casks were emptied'.

SWITZERLAND, as we have seen, sent textiles from the German cantons; from the French, watches.

ITALY sent specimens of the fine arts, and varieties of native stone.

SWEDEN and DENMARK sent Swedish iron, and from Denmark good sculpture and the working model of an electro-magnetic engine. The day had not yet dawned of hydro-electric power, which would swing these countries into the industrial front. Intermediately they were the four with which for the next half century and more it was easiest for Great Britain to be on friendly commercial terms; for they were complementary rather than rival—Denmark and Sweden supplying dairy produce to the wide open mouth of Free-Trade Britain: Italy and Switzerland supplying 'tourism' to the rail-borne travellers from Britain and places beyond.

The court of TUNIS was a pocket edition of the country. TURKEY showed national costumes, carpets, jewelled hookahs. CHINA, too, was treated rather as a joke, apart from its tea; 'The consumption of tea in the United Kingdom is now enormous (in 1850 upwards of 54,000,000 lb.) and it is this little shrub which has succeeded in bringing China into nearer contact with her foreigners than her sages ever desired; for they have ever foreseen, in a free intercourse with other nations the destruction of their own power.' The Chinese exhibits were supplied mainly by the foreign community, British and American. The Chinese Commissioner, asked by the British Plenipotentiary for his support, replied brusquely: 'If men have not the ability to master an art, it is not in the power of their fathers or elder brothers to make them, far less sense would there be in Government addressing them publicly on this head.'[1]

Abruptly THE UNITED STATES closes the foreign section—agricultural as yet rather than industrial; ingenious rather than tasteful; destined to be a great iron-producer, but meanwhile content to exhibit its first trays of Californian gold. Its exhibits had little of the glamour of the Indian treasures but all the fascination of the machine age. The public knew it. As the *Daily News* reported (5 September 1851), interest in the American section was growing daily—especially in Hobb's lock, Colt's revolver, and McCormick's reaping machine. (But Singer's sewing-machine, patented only that year, was conspicuous by its absence.)

Hobb's lock—the ancestor of that triumph of modern production, the Yale—enjoyed adventitious publicity when Mr Hobbs won the challenge money for picking, without damaging, a Bramah lock, product of the famous

[1] Royal Archives: Exhibition of 1851, vol. F 12.

British tool-making firm. The fact that he spread his prize money in sovereigns in front of his exhibit helped to attract even more visitors. His feat soon became proverbial.

Colt's revolver we need say little about. But it was the McCormick reaper,

THE McCORMICK REAPER

harbinger of the revolution in food supply and of the mechanization which was to produce Chicago and Detroit, that was the real portent of the Exhibition. 'It is probable that, within a very short time, similar implements, or some improvement on the American invention, will be very generally used throughout the country. In Agriculture, it appears that the machine will be as important as the spinning-jenny and power-loom in manufactures.'[1] It was a prophetic judgement.

Such then was the Exhibition. Let us remember that this was a spectacle and that tens of thousands of those who saw it had worked in cottage or factory on the products which they saw displayed before them, and had served the machines which were changing them from craftsmen to machine-minders. We to-day might exhibit in model form the history of the evolution, but it would be all past history. For we have not lived in the transition era, with man on the one side of the precipice of time, and the machine on the other.

[1] *Dickinsons' . . . Pictures . . .* , *sub* 'Agricultural Implements' (cf. p. 90 n.).

CHAPTER VI

BENEFITS OF SUCCESS

WHAT was the impact of the Exhibition? Here is the view of a contemporary:

> Everybody knew that the Exhibition had been an 'immense success'; that so far from entailing a call on the Government for pecuniary assistance, a large surplus was in the hands of the Commissioners; everybody had experienced great personal pleasure and profit during an examination of the collections of machines, manufactures or fine art, and felt deeply how useful and interesting, and at the same time, how elevating the spectacle had been to the multitudes who came to study or to admire: everybody had felt it so obligatory to go and see for himself, to gain a knowledge of things of which he was ignorant, to admire in all their perfection, productions with which he was well acquainted, and to compare them with those of other nations, and then to feel that experience had given him a right to praise their excellent points and to decry their deficiencies, and so universal was the affirmative answer to the great question of the day 'Have you been to the Exhibition?' that it became almost possible to point to the solitary individual who would remain blind to the advantages of the undertaking, however patent they might be made to him, and who refused to look upon the whole enterprise in any other light but that of a 'vast humbug'.[1]

'Precisely', chime in critics like Mr Hobhouse, 'it was just a glorious show. It did not bring international peace, it did not improve taste. Imperceptibly it might have promoted free trade; a few manufacturers may have learned from their foreign rivals. That is all, bar an empty building and a large financial surplus.'

[1] *Dickinsons' Comprehensive Pictures of the Great Exhibition of 1851, from the originals painted for H.R.H. Prince Albert by Messrs Nash, Haghe, and Roberts, R.A., published under the Express Sanction of His Royal Highness Prince Albert, President of the Royal Commission, to whom this work is, by permission, dedicated.* In 2 volumes by Dickinson Brothers, 114 New Bond Street, 1854: 'The Closing Ceremony'.

Ought this to be our judgement too? Surely not, for in large and small matters the Great Exhibition has had its effect on British economic history, as on other aspects of British life.

Let us consider, for instance, how British business-men seized the opportunities which it revealed; for it was the first great venture in mass provision for the safety and amusement of the masses. Thus among the six million who visited the Great Exhibition was a Yorkshire lad of farming stock, William Whiteley, whom people came to call 'the universal provider'. It was his twentieth year and his first holiday. As a draper's apprentice he inspected with peculiar interest the silks, linens, damasks and other textiles so beautifully displayed. Why should not London have great shops of this type, bright and open, through which, and outside which, customers might pass in parade? Gas-light and plate-glass were in abundant supply; and since there was then no restriction on shop assistants' hours of work it would be possible to shop till midnight in well-lit streets with well-lit window fronts. He, therefore, migrated to London to master the wholesale side of the business in the employ of Bradbury Greatorex, and after eight years of intense application opened his shop in Westbourne Grove, by Paddington, on 11 March 1863, timing it to the day after the marriage of the Prince of Wales to the Princess Alexandra, when all London would be in a festive mood. Whiteley was the father of the department store. His premises grew, like the early factories, by adding shop to shop, till the time was ripe for rebuilding the cluster in a great and orderly emporium. Royalty patronized his store, and in 1882 he acted as chaperon to ex-King Cetawayo and his black entourage. By this time he boasted he could sell anything from an elephant to a second-hand coffin; if you needed a waiter for your dinner party, the man from Blankley's appeared on your doorstep.

Whiteley's is not the oldest of London's famous shops, nor is it possible to state precisely how far later creations modelled their layout on his. It is, however, certain that he followed the fashion of the Great Exhibition in seeking to attract every range of purse. It is a matter of history that the head of his provisions department, Richard Burbidge, left him to build up Harrods and that he also supplied the men who put John Barker and the Army and Navy Stores on the shopping map.

Even keener to learn the lesson of the Exhibition were the London railway companies. As we have noted, the Great Exhibition came half-way through a great railway-building decade in England, and the masses it set in movement impressed every observer. Its local influence is well seen in the steps which the railway companies took to develop and participate in the Crystal Palace traffic in its second home at Sydenham. Naturally the first in the new field was the London, Brighton and South Coast Railway. For Samuel Laing, the railway's chairman, was chairman of the company which bought the Crystal Palace and took it, along with its valuable name, to Sydenham and re-erected it there (1852-4), with additions. To handle the traffic this railway laid an additional down-line from London Bridge, with a branch coming in from the south-east to the lower limits of the Palace grounds (i.e. to the Low Level Station, as it was later termed). Tickets, including admission to the Palace, could be bought at offices all over London, and there was a special entrance to the departure platform at London Bridge for such ticket-holders. Passengers booking at the station had to present the exact fare, no change being given. The ticket cost 1s. 6d., third-class return, of which the Railway took 5d. and the Palace 1s. 1d. Incidentally, the third-class single from London Bridge to Norwood was 9d.

It was necessary first, however, to get to London Bridge on the south side of the Thames, and this was accomplished by bus or steamer (water-bus, as we are asked to call it now). To handle West End custom the West End of London and the Crystal Palace Junction Railway, from Battersea to the Palace, was authorized, the London Brighton to work it. In 1856 the section from the then wilds of Wandsworth Common to the Palace was finished; and with the opening of Victoria Station, north of the Thames, the route ran from Victoria and Battersea, parallel with the London South Western Railway, to Clapham Common, which thus became Clapham Junction, and from which the West End and Crystal Palace line branched off to Wandsworth and the Crystal Palace.

In the 1860's, the London Chatham and Dover Railway entered the lucrative traffic, coming in from the north and thus reaching the Palace on a level with the building at a terminus consequently named High Level Station; the service was opened on 1 August 1865. This ensured the bilateral competition, so beloved of Victorian railway economy.

What of visitors arriving from the provinces at King's Cross, the London terminus of the Great Northern Railway? To serve these an end-on amalgamation was arranged. In 1864 the London Chatham and Dover had built a costly extension over the Thames to Ludgate Hill (in the City) and Farringdon Street, whence there was a Metropolitan connexion to King's Cross; and accordingly the Great Northern was induced to invest in this extension, to secure direct access to the Crystal Palace traffic.

The success of the Crystal Palace, even on its new site, encouraged rival enterprise elsewhere. Thus in 1862 the following press notice appeared:

Lord Brougham lays the foundation stone of the Palace of the People at Muswell Hill—sponsored by the Great Northern Palace Company—Chairman, Viscount Torrington.

A map shows its strategic location north of the Thames, accessible to a population of 1½ millions. It was designed as a counterpart of the Crystal Palace at Sydenham. Thus Alexandra Palace, 'Ally Pally', was born. The Great Northern Palace Company camouflaged the Great Northern Railway, for none had benefited more from the Exhibition of 1851 than the newly opened Great Northern into King's Cross. Railway enterprise was later systematically to develop seaside resorts: the South-Western, Bournemouth; the Great Western, Torquay. Sydenham and 'Ally Pally' may be regarded as early essays in this form of development.

The Exhibition thus marks an important stage in the evolution of modern British travel. It is, therefore, a piece of historic justice that one of the notable names of British travel was associated with it:

Citizens and visitors of all nations to Chatsworth, Matlock and Derby, by special train from Euston Station tomorrow, July 12 at 1.30 p.m., returning Monday or Tuesday. Fares there and back, 1st class, 17s. 6d.: covered carriages, 12s. 6d. The

93

house and grounds with the magnificent conservatory (the model of the Crystal Palace) of the Duke of Devonshire, will be opened to visitors and the residence and gardens of Joseph Paxton Esq. may be seen. Tickets and particulars may be had at Mr Cook's Midland Excursion office, 14 Seymour Street, Euston Square.

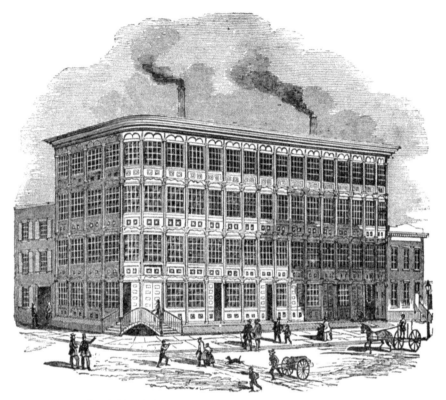

THE FIRST CAST-IRON HOUSE ERECTED IN NEW YORK

Mr Cook was Thomas Cook who won his spurs as an organizer of tourist traffic in the year of the Great Exhibition, as the agent of the Midland Railway for the management of the excursion trade. One of his suggestions was that the railway excursion ticket should include the right of admission to the Exhibition.

These were some results of the Exhibition; but its greatest single achievement, the Crystal Palace, was not without its individual influence. We have already noted its impact on public opinion:

That a Palatial Exhibition building providing a total exhibiting surface of twenty-two acres, and affording space for *nine miles* of tables, shall have been put up in four months, for less than a 1¼*d*. a cubic foot, would in itself make 1851 famous in the history of enterprise, if nothing else were to happen to stamp it as pre-eminently 'the industrial year'. From it will at least be dated a new era in building.[1]

Though the Palace did not, as Charles Dickens's Journal expected, revolutionize architecture, its effect in certain more modest ways may still be seen. Messrs Fox and Henderson constructed a new glass and iron section for an Oxford branch on the same principle as the Crystal Palace. I remember as a boy the glass and iron of certain stations on the Lancashire and Yorkshire railway from Liverpool to Southport. Moreover, Paxton's glasshouses at Chatsworth gave stimulus to glasshouses for fruit and flowers which have survived in mass form in the Lea Valley and other centres of tomato-growing.

Admirably in tune with the age though all these were, they were not the results for which ardent supporters of the Great Exhibition had hoped. These had hoped to erect a monument to progress; they had wished to measure the 'workshop of the world' against the rest of the world; they had seen the Exhibition as a bringer of peace and goodwill:

It is our earnest prayer [wrote Prince Albert] that He who has so far protected an undertaking designed to promote the common good of mankind may give to this that effect which it was intended to produce; and that the Exhibition of 1851 may prove in its results to have been the means of advancing the happiness and prosperity not only of this, but of all other countries, and of strengthening permanently and surely the bonds of peace, of friendship and of brotherhood throughout the world.

How far did the Exhibition achieve these aims? It demonstrated the reality of progress to the satisfaction of contemporaries. Dickens's *Household Words* happily contrasted the marvels of the West with the trivialities of the East, represented by China; progress versus stagnation, represented by gongs and

---

[1] *Household Words*, no. 43, 13 January 1851, 'The Private History of the Palace of Glass'.

95

pigtails and the little lady with her lotus feet. But perhaps the Exhibition exemplified progress most vividly because it confronted Englishmen, emerging from their past, with the new industrial age:

None of the younger generation can realise the sense of novelty it produced in us who were then in our prime. A noun substantive went so far as to become an adjective in honour of the occasion. It was 'exhibition' hat, 'exhibition' razor-strop, 'exhibition' watch; nay, even 'exhibition' weather, 'exhibition' spirits, sweethearts babies, wives—for the time.

For South Wessex the year formed in many ways an extraordinary chronological frontier or transit-line, at which there occurred what one might call a precipice in Time. As in a geological 'fault', we had presented to us a sudden bringing of ancient and modern into absolute contact, such as probably in no other single year since the Conquest was ever witnessed in this part of the country.[1]

British industrial supremacy (though not British taste) could be taken for granted at any rate by most contemporaries. If our industry needed to learn lessons from abroad—and the American exhibitors were already worth watching—others stood in need of more urgent lessons from us. Perhaps the Exhibition did not actually increase our industrial lead. Contemporaries remained satisfied, for it came at the end of decades of economic difficulties, and at the beginning of twenty years of prosperous expansion. That was enough.

What of peace and international understanding? We have seen how strong an argument for the Exhibition was the belief that it could be a great instrument for their achievement. Among the documents in the Royal Archives is one which expresses this feeling, sincere and naïve. It was a set of verses by a Scottish housemaid sent in by a resident of Harrow. These conclude:

> And when we see ower a' the world
> The Flag o' Peace float wide unfurled
> And Wars by Brotherhood down hurled
> We'll laud his name at Harrow.[2]

The Exhibition helped peace and understanding between nations no more

---

[1] Thomas Hardy, *The Fiddler of the Reels.*
[2] Royal Archives: Exhibition of 1851, vol. F 24.

and no less than the Free-Trade movement of which it formed a part. The story of that movement cannot be told here. However, one somewhat unexpected offshoot of these aspirations derived directly from it. On the occasion of the second Exhibition of 1862, which was managed by trustees at the invitation of the Royal Society of Arts and held at South Kensington on the estate acquired by the Commissioners for the Exhibition of 1851, working men of many nations visited England. Socialists from Europe met the trade union *élite* of England. Ferdinand Lassalle came over from Germany to try (unsuccessfully) to make it up with Karl Marx, the exile among the blue books of the British Museum. The outcome of these contacts was the International Working Men's Association of 1864, known later as the First International. From this in due course the Second or Labour and Socialist and the Third or Communist Internationals have derived. Thus internationalism, originating with the exhibition of material goods, was a stepping-stone to the international programme of organized labour.

And yet—what captivated millions was above all the picture of Britain at work. Let us, therefore, ask finally: What did Englishmen carry away from their visits to the Crystal Palace?

Imagine yourself a British worker of 1851. You come up from the provinces to see yourself at work with the tools of your trade in front of you. You feel at home even on buns and lemonade.

You were a Chartist, and your grandson remembers the old Chartist flag, spread across the parlour table. You were a moral-force Chartist in a Scottish Chartist Church, not a physical-force braggart; and therefore you meant business. You jeered at monarchy, not being one of those who sighed for 'the young Queen's picture'. And Tories you detested. Your grandson still has your copy of 'The Tory Profession of Faith':

> I believe that the poor should be slaves of the rich;
> I believe that the Irish should die in a ditch;
> I believe that the East should be ruled by the sword;
> I believe it was made but to profit the Board;[1]

[1] *Sc.* Board of Control for the Affairs of India.

I believe that the peasant should never be taught;
I believe that the patriot but seeks to be bought;
I believe that the system of credit is good;
I believe discontent should be silenced by blood;
I believe that all Government, Lords and M.P.'s
May demand from the country whatever they please;
That a Bishop, who sits as a temporal peer
Should have nothing to do for twelve thousand a year;
And that sailors who sigh for promotion should show
Collateral blood,—not the blood of the foe;
I believe in the good of the National Debt;
I believe that it is not half large enough yet,
And I mean to increase it by what I can get.

You had your '48, and knowing Feargus O'Connor you were not greatly surprised at the outcome, but ten years later, when you heard Professor Playfair lecture at Edinburgh, you laughed to hear him tell the story of his share in the Whitehall patrol on 10 April 1848:

Our orders were peremptory that we were to take into custody any person carrying arms. We met a pretty housemaid with a child of four years of age carrying a drum and tin sword, and, much to the amusement of the former, as well as of the police, we took them into police headquarters. After that we received permission to withdraw.[1]

You did not go to the Great Exhibition but most of your friends did, and you read all about it in your newspaper in the days when a newspaper was a newspaper. You saw that your kind of Chartism was finished. For the time at least 1851 obliterated class feeling. 'Look at this picture of the Queen', said your girls, 'holding the little Prince by the hand and him wearing a Scottish kilt.' They had spent the whole day waiting for a glimpse of the Royal party on their way north to Balmoral. You got a bit tired of Exhibition talk, but you read all about the British Association at Ipswich, and Prince Albert's visit to it. And what were you doing in the later years of your active life?—reading and lecturing on natural science out of a compendium of

[1] *Memoirs,* op. cit. p. 101.

natural history (your grandson still has your Beastie Book) derived from Goldsmith and Buffon. The Prince Consort switched you from sedition to South Kensington, and the *Daily Herald* of your grandson's Labour Party, whatever it may say against capitalism, will take nothing but pleasure in the Duke and Duchess of Edinburgh.

Or again, imagine yourself a member of the middle class. You were a Manchester man, and the completeness of your victory in 1846 left you rather breathless. But it was good for you to lose your inferiority complex (for such at bottom your anti-landlordism was) and to take hold—to co-operate with London under a chairman who was more at home with you and men of science than he was with the Horse Guards or with huntin' and shootin'. You therefore sent Cobden to Paris in 1860, by which time Cobden himself had learnt that there were uses for a Granville or a Clarendon. But one disservice the Exhibition did you, and it is the danger of all Exhibitions, which from their nature present the world at a moment of time. It made you think that the East was yours for all time. You forgot that your own cotton industry was itself the outcome of a ruthless protection against the sub-continent which you were flooding now with Manchester goods. The Indian display of 1851 derived its momentum from a crumbling past. Your guide, your Free-Trade guide, told you that India no longer had an aptitude for manufacture, or at any rate had a less aptitude than yours: and that she was destined to send henceforth not merely or mainly luxuries like calicoes, silks and precious stones, but staple foodstuffs and raw materials, wheat, cotton, oil seeds, manganese, jute and tea. But it fell out otherwise. India, moving towards independence, achieved an industrial renaissance, to which you contributed and can contribute (though in a way you did not then suspect) for many years to come, namely in the supply of machinery of all sorts, including textile machinery itself.

Finally, imagine yourself a University man. Perhaps this very year you went up to Balliol or Trinity College, Cambridge. Perhaps you were only just born. It is less the display at the Crystal Palace that impresses you, than the schemes for education and improvement which sprang from it and which we shall discuss in the next chapter. You are an Arnold Toynbee and you will inspire that great foundation in the East End, Toynbee Hall, the parent of many other University and school settlements in London and elsewhere. I shall seem to speak fancifully if I regard these settlements as the complement of the Natural Science Institutions of the West End. But Toynbee Hall and South Kensington had this in common, that they did not allow their good work to be thwarted by sectarian religion. The Universities of Oxford and Cambridge achieved their renaissance from within, but undoubtedly they were helped and invigorated by their contacts with the metropolis in social and scientific affairs. This broadening of the horizon of the Universities may also be regarded as a result of the Great Exhibition; a welcome one, for the Universities still have a major part to play in the life of the country.

CHAPTER VII

SOUTH KENSINGTON

WHAT meanwhile was happening to the Exhibition itself? The first problem was how to dispose of the Crystal Palace. It had become part of London's life. Mr Punch was as distressed as Her Majesty to observe the dismantling:

When we saw the auctioneer's placards desecrating or rather staining the glass of the Great Exhibition building, we felt a sort of curdling of the blood—a kind of figurative conversion of it into cold cream—at the idea of our pet-palace being besieged by the broadsides of the bill-stickers. When we observed the word Materials in gigantic letters, announced to be knocked down by the hammer of the auctioneer, we thought the public were ninny-hammers themselves for not protesting against the sad sacrifice.[1]

Others felt like *Punch* and sympathized with its attempt to save the Palace:

A Crystal Palace of its own New York's to have, I see,
And another, too, in Paris erected is to be.
But after all, I hope and trust it's not to disappear;
They'll surely never pull it down—Do you think
            they will, my dear?[2]

And again:

And now the elegant destructors of Hyde Park propose to have their First of May. People of England, swear yourselves into yourselves—as special constables to preserve this Crystal Palace.[3]

The fate of the Palace preoccupied not only the public but also the Government—as did that of Prince Albert's model lodgings for working men which Lord Shaftesbury wanted moved to the Zoo, there to accommodate some Board of Health employees.[4]

[1] *Punch*, vol. XXII, p. 113.   [2] Ibid. p. 155.   [3] Ibid. p. 186.
[4] Royal Archives: Exhibition of 1851, vol. F 25.

On 10 August 1851, Prince Albert opposed the suggestion to turn it into a Winter Garden as unlikely to meet the purpose of the Exhibition surplus, friendship between nations.[1]

However, since Parliament had pledged itself to occupy Hyde Park only temporarily, it could not keep the Palace there. Henry Cole agitated for its removal to Battersea, more accessible to London as a whole and to the West End by the new Chelsea Bridge.[1] The Prime Minister, Lord Derby, reported to the Prince on an offer from a private company to purchase the Palace, if they could get a site 'in the newly sanctioned Battersea Park'. The Prince assented.[1]

The rest of the story may be told in two reports to the Queen and the Prince Consort:

Disraeli to the Queen

The Chancellor of the Exchequer, with his humble duty to your Majesty reports to your Majesty that Mr Heywood's motion, in favour of retaining the Crystal Palace, has been negatived by a majority of 221 against 103.

The House was very noisy throughout the night, but good-humoured. Ld Palmerston misjudged the temper of the House, and wishing to have the appearance of deciding the question, rose late in the evening and made the mistake of declaring for the motion. The speech of the evening was made by Ld Seymour, who was greatly effective and greatly influenced the result.

Grey to the Prince   ST JAMES'S PALACE
                                                                        12 *May* 1852

Sir,

I have just seen Mr Cole and I think yr. R.H. will like to hear at once the intelligence he gives me that the Crystal Palace has been bona fide purchased for £70,000, and the whole of the money actually paid today. The Chairman of the Brighton Railway is the chairman of the Coy. who have purchased it,—it is to be transferred to Sydenham in Kent where it will be re-erected entire with such additions as may appear desirable. Messrs Owen Jones and Digby Wyatt are engaged to superintend the work, and the Brighton Railway Co., it is said, guarantee to the speculators, on condition of its being erected on their railway, 6 per cent on a capital not exceeding £500,000.

[1] Royal Archives: Exhibition of 1851, vol. F 25.

And in Sydenham the Palace stood until its destruction by fire in 1936, enlarged, rebuilt and supplied by Digby Wyatt with a series of courts, Pompeian, Byzantine, Gothic, Renaissance and Elizabethan. There its remains stand to this day.

The disposal of the Palace was a minor problem, that of the Exhibition surplus of £186,000 a major one. Albert's own ideas on the subject were precise:

Memorandum by the Prince Consort (undated) *August* 1851

[In contrast with France and its Central School of Arts and Manufactures] I find that in England the separate pursuits of industry are represented by a variety of public societies struggling for existence unconnected with each other, and either unprovided with suitable locations or exhausting in providing them the funds which should be applied to the promotion of their respective objects. Could not such societies, or most of them, containing as they do all that this country possesses of talent and experience in these branches, be induced to unite in this institution, reserving to each its individuality and self-supporting and self-maintaining character, but bringing them together under a common roof?[1]

The Prince's idea was to buy thirty to fifty acres in Kensington Gore, mainly from Baron Villars, which were believed to be on sale, to put on them four institutions, corresponding to the four great sections of the Exhibition —raw materials, machinery, manufactures, plastic arts—and to use any surplus for a central garden with conservatory. The learned societies were to be grouped into one great institution of which contributors to the Exhibition would be life members.[2]

Among the Prince's friends the scheme was popular. 'Now', wrote Phipps to Playfair, 'is the time to ask the Societies to accept centralisation.' The Prince, however, drew the line at including the Royal Society. He rejected the suggestion that the Exhibition Commissioners should provide accommodation for it, for, as he wrote to Lord John Russell, 'To give the surplus away, in order to provide with better accommodation a Society which, as at

[1] Royal Archives: Exhibition of 1851, vol. F 25.
[2] Memorandum by Prince Consort on use of Exhibition surplus, 10 August 1851. Royal Archives, vol. F 25.

present constituted, has forfeited the sympathy of the generality of the public by its lethargic state and exclusive principles, cannot I am sure be thought of for a moment.'[1]

There was bound to be political opposition to the purchase of the South Kensington estate, but it was minimized by adopting a suggestion of the then Chancellor of the Exchequer, Benjamin Disraeli. Once again we will let the documents tell their own story.[1]

Disraeli to the Prince
H. OF C.

Thursday, 10 *June*

Sir,

I have the honour and satisfaction to report to Yr. Royal Highness that I have succeeded in making with the Governors of the Bank the arrangement which I took the liberty of suggesting to yr. R.H. and which yr. R.H. approved.

The arrangement will be kept secret. Any partial and ill-timed disclosure of the great project is now rendered unnecessary, and yr. R.H. will be enabled to introduce it to the nation in that complete form and at that happy moment, which become the vast and beautiful conception.

That, when realised, the creation of yr. R.H. will form an epoch in the aesthetic and scientific education of the people of England is the conviction of yr. R.H's
Most humble and obedient servant.

B. DISRAELI

Memo. by Governor of Bank of England
9 *June* 1852

The Bank of England will be willing to lend £110,000 on the terms above mentioned at the mortgage rate of 3½ p.c. per annum, the securities being approved by their solicitors.

The Prince to Ld Derby

... Mr Cubitt[2] is going to bid Baron V's ground. May God speed him, that he may not have to pay too much!

The Prince to Ld Derby

Baron Villars has accepted our offer of £150,000.

---

[1] Royal Archives: Exhibition of 1851, vol. F 25.
[2] Thomas Cubitt presumably, for William was now Sir William Cubitt.

Ld Derby to the Prince

I hope I may be allowed to congratulate yr. R.H. on the Villars 'Capitulation'. I hope that in conjunction with Mr Walpole I have come to terms with the Crystal Palace Company, such as will be satisfactory to them, and dispose of the very difficult question of Sunday opening and Sunday trains; and if they carry out their present intentions, yr. R.H. will have the satisfaction, not only of having carried out with perfect success the wonderful experiment of the original building, but of having led to the establishment of an Institution, perfectly unparalleled in its scope and design, and calculated to confer lasting benefits, of the highest character, on the population of the Metropolis.

Extract from the Queen's speech   *11 November* 1852

The advancement of the Fine Arts and of Practical Science will be readily recognised by you, as worthy of the attention of a great and enlightened nation. I have directed that a comprehensive Scheme shall be laid before you, having in view the Promotion of these Objects, towards which I invite your aid and co-operation.

Disraeli to the Queen   *6 December* 1852

The Chancellor of the Exchequer with his humble duty to Yr. Majesty reports to Yr. Majesty with great gratification, that the vote for the purchase of land at Kensington Gore was carried unanimously this evening though after a protracted, and at one time, somewhat perilous discussion. . . .

What precisely was to be done with land and funds?

The 1852 Report of the Royal Commissioners gives us a clear picture of what was in Albert's mind—the cause for which Henry Cole was to fight on after the Prince's death. Nor should it be forgotten that it was Disraeli's cause too. As he wrote to the Prince in 1858:

I need not assure yr. R.H. that I have never, for a moment, in or out of office, swerved from those views which yr. R.H. deigned to develop to me, when I first had the honour of being placed in confidential relations to yr. R.H., and the entire fulfilment of which I believe to be alike necessary to the intellectual progress and the material prosperity of this country.[1]

[1] 5 March 1858. Royal Archives: Exhibition of 1851, vol. F 25.

Indeed, from first to last, in all the Exhibition and South Kensington correspondence with the Prince Consort and Queen Victoria, Gladstone's stock falls and Disraeli's rises. In our history of public finance we barely note, except to smile, that Disraeli was twice Chancellor of the Exchequer. His office on each occasion was brief but he used it to help forward, to the best of his powers, the cause that was central to the designs of the Prince and therefore to the wishes of the Queen. And Queen Victoria never forgot.

The main use of the surplus was to be the promotion of industrial education and the application of science and art to productive industry. The Report of the Commission in 1852 recommended the founding of a central institution and the dissemination of its services by the award of scholarships to students from the provinces and colonies. There they were to learn 'the lesson of the Continent', where trade schools and industrial universities taught people how to become intelligent manufacturers, an education completed by training in the industrial works. Prince Albert had already inaugurated lectures on the lessons of the Exhibition, showing how lack of scientific instruction had cramped British industry.[1]

The Commission's task was to provide a *system* and a *locality*, leaving the rest to Government and private enterprise. All the various institutions were to be, if possible, grouped on the South Kensington estates. Attention was to be confined to technical instruction: foreign students were to be received on an equal footing. This technical instruction was not intended to replace workshop experience but to supplement it; and the Commission keenly urged manufacturers to recognize the greater potential activity of the college-educated man, once he had practical experience. The surgeon, as Playfair argued, must have hospital practice after leaving the lecture-room, but he is the better surgeon for having had lecture-room instruction first.

[1] They were delivered before the Royal Society of Arts (Whewell, the Master of Trinity, opening the series) and published in volume form in 1852. Lyon Playfair took as his subject the application of science to industry. De la Beche lectured on mining; Richard Owen on raw materials from the animal kingdom; Robert Willis on machines and tools, etc. I think that henceforth Applied Science meant more to the Prince than Applied Art, which was the nostrum of Henry Cole and the Royal Society of Arts.

Not all the Prince's hopes were realized, though in the early 1850's prospects seemed bright. Lord John Russell, however, uttered a note of caution:

The scientific teaching and collections should all be ancillary to the great purposes of Art, etc.—thereby distinguishing the institution from the Royal Society, Cambridge, where the objects are purely scientific. . . . The old gentlemen of our scientific societies will be very apt to grumble if they are put out of their way for their evening meetings and quiet elections.

Indeed, as Playfair wrote to Grey: 'The Societies are dead against us now, but for that I care nothing.'

At this stage, public opinion, as represented by the newspapers, still seemed favourable. Playfair noted that Delane of *The Times* approved of the general principles of industrial instruction. *The Times*, however, was not to remain so friendly:

The conduct of the *Times* [wrote Granville to the Prince some years later] is abominable. . . . Whatever may be the unworthy object, this sort of attack is an evil. The *Times* is like the King of Naples who is hated, but is feared and obeyed in his own country. . . . I believe the two most important persons are Walter and Delane. The first I am told is all powerful when he interferes. I do not know him, but I am informed that he is narrow-minded and violent, rather a morbid, but not a bad man. . . . Delane is vulgar, without much appearance of ability, but must understand his own trade. He seems very open to personal civility.[1]

More serious than the opposition of the societies were the difficulties of politics. As usual with proposals for educational change, religion raised its head. As early as 1851 the Prince had warned Playfair to beware of accusations of 'godless institutions' from the religious world. Still, as Granville told the Prince, his plan had political advantages. Since religious feeling would prevent any national plan for education 'therefore yr. R.H.'s suggestions with reference to scientific instruction ought to be a godsend to the Government'.[2]

The Prince answered Granville that Gladstone was prepared to support

[1] Granville to the Prince, Carlsbad, 5 July 1856. Royal Archives: Exhibition of 1851, vol. F 25.
[2] Granville to the Prince, 14 January 1854. Royal Archives: Exhibition of 1851, vol. F 25.

the establishment of the Department of Practical Science, but to minimize the danger of religious outcry thought it ought to be in the Board of Trade, and not in the Office of the Privy Council. He understood the Board of Trade was to be remodelled. Granville regretted this, in view of the multifarious duties of the Board of Trade, but admitted that the religious squabble argument was decisive.[1]

Parliament, however, was lacking in enthusiasm. Friendly though Disraeli was, Gladstone appears to have had neither understanding of nor sympathy for the Prince's project. Albert was horrified when he endorsed Sir Charles Trevelyan's suggestion to appropriate the eastern outlying portion of the Kensington estate to the erection of barracks on the grounds of economy:

You not only deprive the Commissioners of the best slice of their ground, but that which was peculiarly adapted for the different learned societies should they be inclined to seek a habitation in this locality—but from the effect which the neighbourhood of a barrack always has in deteriorating the value of the neighbouring property (from a perhaps not unreasonable dread of the description of dwellings and inhabitants that are usually found in the vicinity of a barrack) you run a serious risk of permanently damaging a scheme, which has yet to be arrived at.[2]

Moreover, Gladstone was, to say the least of it, unhelpful in the fight for two schemes—one sponsored by the Prince himself, the other after his death very much in the Prince's spirit. These were the plan to transfer the National Gallery from Trafalgar Square to South Kensington in 1853-8 (and the later plan to separate the Natural History Museum from the British Museum), and the proposal to purchase the land and buildings of the 1862 Exhibition for the Department of Science and Art.[3]

Parliamentary opposition to the former scheme eventually created a deadlock which led to the termination of the partnership between the Government and the Royal Commissioners in 1858:

I have never been able to understand the bitterness existing in the House against our Commission, for having endeavoured to help it and the Government in their

---

[1] Granville to the Prince, 14 January 1854. Royal Archives: Exhibition of 1851, vol. F 25.
[2] The Prince to Gladstone. Royal Archives: Exhibition of 1851, vol. F 25.
[3] See Appendix II for documents from the Royal Archives relating to these transactions.

objects, and now again for trying to free them from engagements of which they had complained as onerous and irksome.[1]

The Prince's friends resented Parliamentary opposition. Thus Granville wrote:

The only thing which has been bad for my 'cure' was the report of the debate in the H. of C. on the Kensington Gore estate. It irritated me so much that I was kept awake the whole night . . . the two points which ought to endear you the most to all Englishmen are your great liberality in political opinions and the manner in which you have identified yourself with English interests. The small clique who attempt to diminish the appreciation by the nation of all that you have done, know that their only chance is to try and represent your R.H. as averse to English habits and institutions. . . .[2]

At bottom, however, the opposition to the South Kensington scheme was of the same sort as beset other great administrative centralizers and reformers in the 1840's and 1850's—the same that destroyed Chadwick's Board of Health. It was one which neither the Prince nor his supporters ever fully understood.

To what extent, then, has the Prince's great scheme been achieved? The history of technical education and industrial design cannot be told here. We can, however, briefly survey the concrete embodiment of the Prince's plan, the South Kensington estate.

The original estate comprised 87 acres. Of these 18 acres have been absorbed by the construction of roadways, 17 acres have been appropriated as sites for residential houses, and 52 acres have been devoted to public buildings. The Government have acquired possession of about 40 acres, or 70 per cent of the area assigned to public use, at a price (£250,000) which represents less than one-fifth of the value of the bare land. The whole of the remaining 12 acres are leased to educational institutions at nominal rents. The Estate's limits are: in the north Kensington Road facing Hyde Park, in the south Cromwell Road and Brompton Road, in the east Exhibition Road and in the west Queen's Gate.

[1] The Prince to Disraeli. Royal Archives: Exhibition of 1851, vol. F25.
[2] Royal Archives: Exhibition of 1851, vol. F25.

If not all the institutions are here that Albert would have wished to see, quite a lot of them are. Though learned societies were shy of coming to South Kensington, the Physical Society and the Royal Geographical Society are there, however, as are the Royal College of Organists and the Royal College of Music.

More important, however, than these are the two other educational institutions on the estate and its four great museums: the Royal College of Art and the Imperial College of Science on the one hand, the Victoria and Albert, the Geological, the Natural History and the Science Museums on the other.

Let us glance at these institutions and at the history of scientific and artistic education which they embody.

ROYAL COLLEGE OF ART

The genesis of the Royal College of Art was the School of Design opened at Somerset House in 1837, in pursuance of the Report of the Select Committee on Arts and Manufactures of 1836. It was to teach 'ornamental' as distinguished from 'fine' art: and in the next room to it were objects of decorative art, which came via Marlborough House to the Victoria and Albert Museum. No progress was made till local schools were started, after which the Government School became the *Central* School of Design, and its function increasingly the training of teachers for local schools. Renamed Central School of Art, and finally in 1897 Royal College of Art, it was not till recently that its original purpose, teaching and research in practical design, was resumed and realized; and this for three reasons: (1) the need for art teachers was clamant; (2) distinguished Principals, who were also distinguished artists, such as Sir Edward Poynter and Sir William Rothenstein, naturally stressed the fine arts; (3) Henry Cole, who most clearly visualized its distinctive function, was, unhappily for himself and the progress of Science, placed in a position as Inspector General of the Science and Art Department, which brought him into conflict with the scientists and finally into political disfavour. But to-day at long last the Royal College of Art is assuming the role which he and the Prince Consort designed for it.

PLATE XVI

THE ALBERT MEMORIAL

IMPERIAL COLLEGE OF SCIENCE

This College is made up of three constituent bodies: the Royal School of Mines, the Royal College of Science, and the City and Guilds College.

ROYAL SCHOOL OF MINES

In the science group the senior partner is the school of mines, which was associated at its birth with geology. 'Born in 1851 of the Geological Survey and Sir Henry de la Beche, the Prince Consort standing sponsor and patron', it was housed in whole or part in Jermyn Street for the first thirty years of its life—the period of the so-called 'Thirty Years' War'. But this is now past history. To-day the Royal School of Mines, reassembled in South Kensington, 'provides specialized instruction nominally only in Mining and Metallurgy, but actually also in Mining Geology and Oil Technology: thus we are returning to our old natural association with Geology' (and, as will be seen, the Geological Museum is now in South Kensington also). Thus runs the official history.[1] De la Beche organized the mining school around the Geological Survey, which Peel had separated from its ordnance colleague, grouping into one unit the Survey, the Museum and the Mining Record Office. When the Prince Consort was appointed Chancellor of the University of Cambridge, Adam Sedgwick, the Professor of Geology there, became his secretary and this inclined H.R.H. to the new institution, whose home in Jermyn Street he opened on 12 May 1851 under the style of Museum of Practical Geology, 'the first palace ever raised from the ground in Britain, which is entirely devoted to the achievement of Science'. 'Palace' is an echo of 'Crystal Palace', with the opening of which its own opening was timed, and it was designed as a centre of continuous practical work by contrast with the Royal Society and Royal Institution, which were places of meeting, lectures and high research. Having got his Museum, de la Beche expanded it into a 'School of Mines and of Science applied to Arts'. This brought lecture courses at Jermyn Street in chemistry from Lyon Playfair and in natural history from Edward Forbes,

[1] *Register and History of the Royal School of Mines*, by Margaret Reeks (1920). The Geological Department of the Royal College of Science is located to-day (1949) in the Royal School of Mines.

whom Huxley shortly succeeded. Playfair lectured on chemistry as applied to agriculture, Forbes on botany and zoology as applied to geology and the arts. Specialist pupils at first were few, but the evening lectures were thronged by fascinated audiences of artisans.

That a metropolitan school of science should start as a school of mines, resting on geology, was natural to a country which was itself rich in mineral resources and also had overseas possessions where new fields of study were constantly opening out. Not as yet styled 'imperial', it was in principle imperial, as was the parallel development in natural history, through the work of Banks, Darwin, Huxley and others in the coastal waters of formal or informal empire. The admiralty surveys went hand in hand with the ordnance surveys. Both contributed to the national defence, and both, therefore, even in a *laisser-faire* age, secured Government support. Furthermore, coal-mining called for remedies against waste and accidents, and this likewise made a call on Government. The incentive to the collection of mining records came from the British Association meeting at Newcastle in 1838, and the Prince Consort on behalf of the Duchy of Cornwall promptly deposited its records with them.

Mining led on to metallurgy; and John Percy made himself at Birmingham the father of English metallurgy. As Professor at the Royal School of Mines he had among his pupils the famous Sidney Gilchrist Thomas. Percy and others were loth to leave Jermyn Street and be separated from their Museum, but circumstances were too strong for them. There was no place there for necessary extensions, and the Royal School of Mines was transferred by stages to South Kensington, first the affiliated Departments of Biology and Physics, then that of Chemistry, then Geology (1877) and Metallurgy (1880), followed in 1934 by the Museum itself.

ROYAL COLLEGE OF SCIENCE

Though formally equated with Art at the outset in the single Department of Science and Art, applied science was much too potent to develop only *pari passu*. For applied science, when seriously tackled, meant general science;

and general science by the end of the century had become in the secondary schools of the country a subject with a range which art could not match, except in its broad sense of the humanities, embracing classics, languages, history and fine art. One headwater of science teaching was, as we have seen, the School of Mines in Jermyn Street. A second, smaller but older stream was the Royal College of Chemistry, established in 1845 and housed in 1846 in Oxford Street. Though its resources were inadequate, it was able to attract W. von Hoffman (1845-65). England was indebted to the Prince Consort for introducing to England not only Hoffman, but also on occasion the greater figures of Liebig and Bunsen, such scholars being regarded by nervous natives as evidence of the German invasion. In 1853, with Hoffman as Professor, the College of Chemistry was incorporated in the Government's 'Metropolitan School of Science applied to Mining and the Arts', of which in 1853 Huxley became the Professor of Geology in succession to Edward Forbes. Between 1854 and 1881 general science was an uneasy attachment to the School of Mines. But in 1881 the two separated; and thenceforth the Royal School of Mines and the Normal School of Science, as it was now called, developed side by side, with T. H. Huxley as Dean of the whole. But 'normal school', taken from the École Normale of Paris, was less happy than the other word with which Huxley enriched the language—'agnostic', and so in 1890 the title was changed to Royal College of Science; but the School of Mines, proud of its tradition, continued to be a school, though a Royal School, and is so to this day. The significance of Huxley's tenure as Professor of Biology and Dean of the College was threefold:

(1) Huxley in Biology like Tyndall in Physics[1] (Tyndall moving later to the Royal Institution) fought the battle of evolutionary science in opposition to the addicts of miracles. Huxley was the gladiator of Darwin; the *Origin of Species* was his bible, and he loved a fray as much as Darwin detested it.

[1] H. E. Armstrong, with a veteran record as Professor of Chemistry at City and Guilds, wrote of Huxley and Tyndall (he was staying at the time at Hodelsea, Huxley's old home): 'Huxley and Ramsay might have been gramophone records, they set the modern fashion of retailing textbooks. . . but by John Tyndall the Irishman (1820-93) wave motion was made actual before our eyes; heat, too, was shown in motion. . . . I can still visualise every detail of Tyndall's demonstration.' (*The Central*, vol. xxxv, no. 83, June 1938.)

(2) Huxley came to the front as a national figure at a time when a man of genius could master the whole range of 'ologies' (including anthropology) comprised under natural history. He achieved in the field of science what his intellectual opposite, W. E. Gladstone, achieved in the field of finance: he made the nation feel that they understood it in whole as well as in some detail. And in his appeal to the working classes he came, I think, midway between the Mechanics Institutes and the Workers' Educational Association.

(3) And specifically, in 1872, when the general science departments had been established on an independent footing at South Kensington, it was possible to do there what other leading Universities also were by way of doing, namely, 'to establish a system of science teaching based upon laboratory work by the students'.[1]

CITY AND GUILDS COLLEGE

The City and Guilds College, a more recent foundation, does not name itself by its function; if it did it would be 'Royal College of Engineering'. But the founders had in mind the problem of technical education as a whole, and this concern is reflected in the full title of the federal body—Imperial College of Science and Technology. (In any case 'College of Engineering' was pre-empted by the Royal Engineering College at Cooper's Hill, near Staines, which ran from 1871 to 1906.) Furthermore, its original purpose was not so precise; for it was the outcome of the determination of the Corporation and Livery Companies of the City of London to promote technical education.[2]

One great figure runs through its history: William Cawthorne Unwin, 1838-1933, Professor of (Civil and Mechanical) Engineering, 1884-1904. Before that he was Instructor at the Royal School of Naval Architecture and Marine Engineering in South Kensington, which later went to Greenwich. Shortly after the Government established its college for the training of engineers for the public services in India he became its Professor of Hydraulic

---

[1] L. Huxley, *Life and Letters of T. H. Huxley*, vol. II, p. 81.

[2] The first move was the Finsbury Technical College, 1889; the second the Central Institution of the City and Guilds of London Institute, renamed in 1893 Central Technical College, and finally in 1907 City and Guilds College (but its Old Boys are still 'Centralians').

Engineering, 1872-85; then he returned to South Kensington once more, where he built up the engineering college. The closure of Cooper's Hill, 1906, was due to the growth of engineering instruction not only in South Kensington, but also in new schools in the provinces, and the mechanization of the Indian engineering service was an additional reason.

Unwin's influence on the City and Guilds College was big—not only by reason of his length of service (for he was a foundation member, professor for twenty years, and for many years thereafter engaged in private research work there), but also because he combined great practical experience with great theoretical knowledge:

He wrote books which were the standard treatises of their time, used more as handbooks in engineers' offices than as textbooks of instruction. His *Treatise on Hydraulics* (in its first form an *Encyclopaedia Britannica*, 1881, Article) was the authoritative basis for the development of Indian irrigation and river control works for more than a generation. In its successive editions his book on machine design was almost universally used in British drawing offices for half a century, and was also used extensively abroad.[1]

To crown all he was a leading consultant on hydro-electric development in Niagara and south India, and on the merits of the petroleum (Ackroyd-Stewart, Diesel) engine.

It came to me as a pleasure to read in his Life that his first work as a young man in the service of Sir William Fairbairn was to report on the merits of my grandfather's railway break (then so spelt). I have read the report in the City and Guilds Library, which is introduced by a covering letter from Sir John Aspinall, General Manager of the Lancashire and Yorkshire Railway, 25 November 1919: 'Dear Mr Unwin, I think it might interest you to read once again a report which you drafted, and which Fairbairn signed, about the Fay and Newall breaks.' The trials between the two chain breaks were conducted in 1859, first on the Oldham Incline (outside Manchester)—my father was present at this—and then on the Liverpool and Southport line between Ainsdale and Birkdale. Unwin was in the guard's van to see fair play, for the

[1] From the I.C.E. Council appreciation, quoted in E. G. Walker's *Life and Work of William Cawthorne Unwin*, p. 175.

feeling, as he notes, between the two parties was tense. The upshot was that my grandfather and Mr Newall pooled their ideas, embodying in the Fay and Newall break certain of the suggestions made by Mr Unwin. After a run of some years, the break was ousted by the pneumatic break of George Westinghouse. But how great an advance the continuous chain break was on the old detached hand breaks is eloquently set out in Unwin's closing paragraph:

On most through lines the train reaches 60 miles an hour and in the event of an obstruction perceived at half a mile in advance, as may easily happen, a collision is inevitable unless the driver acts with extreme promptitude; at 60 miles an hour there are only 30 seconds to effectuate the breaking of the train, and it is impossible with their present condition to stop or retard the train before it is in actual collision. Assuming, however, that self-acting breaks upon the principle of Mr Newall and Mr Fay were attached to both engine and train, the driver having the power of instantaneous application by releasing a spring, even in such a precarious position, instead of rushing to destruction, the whole momentum of the train might be destroyed in a distance of less than 500 yards, and the injury to life and property prevented. The application of the electric telegraph in preventing more than one train being on the same line between two given points is a great additional security, and this, united with a more perfect system of signals, together with the employment of adequate break power by continuous breaks applied to the train and to the engine, render collisions less frequent if not next to impossible.

I have the honour to be,
Gentlemen,
Your faithful and obedient servant
WM. FAIRBAIRN

MANCHESTER, 30 *June* 1859.

ROYAL COLLEGE OF MUSIC

Its situation is correct. For it is on the Prince Consort Road, facing the Exhibition Memorial and the Albert Hall. Its north-south line, projected, passes through the centre of the Imperial Institute, and over against it is the headquarters of the Imperial College of Science. The Prince had an intellectual urge to applied science, but his heart was in music and the arts and in the greatness of his adopted country.

Founded by the Prince of Wales in 1882 and opened by him 7 May 1883, the Royal College is one of the two national schools of music, the other being the older Royal Academy of Music in York Gate, Marylebone Road. The purposes of the sister foundations are similar, namely to advance the art of music by a central examining and teaching body; to promote musical teaching in the schools, and music in the Dominions generally. If there is a difference, it lies perhaps in the greater emphasis which the Academy now lays on elocution. Negotiations for the amalgamation of the two bodies have been made more than once, but the older body was unwilling to move to South Kensington at the outset, and the site granted later by the Commissioners of 1851 for a Training School of Music (1873) is occupied now by an examining body, the Royal College of Organists, founded in 1864 and incorporated by Royal Charter in 1893.

Great musicians have held office both at the Royal College of Music and at the Royal Academy of Music: George Grove, Hubert Parry, Hugh Allen and George Dyson at the one, Sterndale Bennett, Alexander Mackenzie, Henry Wood at the other. Sir George Dyson has said of Hubert Parry: 'There was something in the artistic background of living and encyclopaedic scholarship which Parry may be said to have embodied, which made the College in those days a place of vivid and intimate artistic ideals.' And Parry, like William Morris, was of Exeter College, Oxford. We who have spent our academic life at Cambridge know how the specialization of studies there has been counterbalanced by the renaissance of music and drama, so nobly illustrated in the Arts Theatre of Lord Keynes. Science had to divide itself in order to take the strain, now it is engaged in trying to reassemble itself; and the effort is part of a wider urge to the reunion of the human mind, to which music contributes its harmony. This again is splendidly faithful to the ideals of the Prince Consort.

THE MUSEUMS

VICTORIA AND ALBERT MUSEUM

The Victoria and Albert Museum of to-day—the South Kensington of yesterday—adjoins the Royal School of Art, but is quite separate from it in

respect of organization and activity. It has its own art library and lecture
theatre, and it plays a greater part proportionately in the total art effort than
do the other museums in the whole science effort. It dates officially from 1852,
but, just as in geology there was a Craig's Court before Jermyn Street, so in
art there was a collection of art objects at Somerset House, in connexion with
the Government School of Design, before the opening in 1852 of the Museum
of Manufactures on the first floor of Marlborough House. In this royal
residence were housed the collections from Somerset House, and in addition
the objects bought from the Great Exhibition with the noble sum of £5000
voted by the Government for purchasing therefrom objects of applied art
'to be selected without reference to styles but entirely for the excellence of
their workmanship'. The Museum expanded with further purchases and loans
from private collections, and since Marlborough House would be needed by
the Prince of Wales when he came of age, the Government in 1857 decided
to assemble in South Kensington the contents of Marlborough House (Art
Library and Museum of Ornamental Art), the British paintings from the
newly presented Sheepshanks collection, and a miscellany of exhibits based
on the classification of the 1851 Exhibition. It was opened in 1857 under the
title of South Kensington Museum. The buildings were of iron, and known
popularly as the Brompton Boilers (removed subsequently to Bethnal
Green where they now stand as the Bethnal Green Museum); and in
front was a small Patent Museum, in temporary quarters only. But these
occupied only a small part of the ground now covered by the Victoria
and Albert.

In 1899 the foundation stone of the new and present museum was laid by
Queen Victoria—her last public ceremony: and ten years later, on 26 June
1909, the 'Victoria and Albert', as it was now styled, was opened by King
Edward VII. It was now for the first time a purely art museum. Since
nearly everyone has walked through its galleries, I will not attempt to
describe it. But I lay stress on its metropolitan stature. It has 'outstations'
in Bethnal Green, Apsley House and Ham House near Richmond. In the
language of the *Official Guide*:

As the Museum is a part of the Ministry of Education, it is possible to keep in the closest touch with educational bodies, art schools and training colleges throughout the country, and the long standing connection with the Royal College of Art, as well as relations with industry, ensures that the 'application of the arts to manufactures' is also fostered by the Victoria and Albert Museum.

On the staircase of the Museum is a mosaic of Henry Cole (1808-82), and the inscription reads: 'Erected to record the eminent services of Sir Henry Cole, K.C.B., who, in addition to other labours in the promotion of Science and Art, devoted twenty years to the foundation of this Museum.' This, indeed, is where he is most fittingly remembered. Prince Albert on 15 October 1851, in forwarding to him an Exhibition Medal, wrote: 'You have been one of the few who originated the design, became its exponent and fought its battles in adversity, and belong now to those who share in its triumphs.'

He was not popular with the scientists, and his zeal sometimes outran his discretion, but he kept before him to the end the central purpose of the Prince Consort—so much so, that he seemed the Prince's other self.

GEOLOGICAL MUSEUM

This museum with its subtitle, Museum of Practical Geology, is more closely related than any of the others to a single branch of knowledge, but just as the Natural History Museum had incidental contacts with naval expeditions, so the Geological Museum had formal contacts with military ordnance. The story must be told around the Geological Survey.

The foundation in 1807 of the Geological Society of London assembled a body of distinguished men and to these the Ordnance Board naturally turned in 1835 when inviting geologists to combine a geological examination of the English counties with the geographical survey then in progress. This was to invite them to continue what one of their brotherhood had engaged upon already as a private venture, William Smith, 1769-1839, the founder of stratigraphical geology. The Chancellor of the Exchequer backed the request, and a Treasury grant defrayed the cost incurred in colouring geographically the ordnance county maps. Thus was born the Geological Survey, which celebrated its centenary in 1935, the year in which the Geological Museum was moved to its present home in South Kensington. At the instance of de la Beche, the first director of the Geological Survey, a museum was formed to house the specimens sent in by workers on the Survey, and to these he added specimens of the different types of building stone under examination for the new Houses of Parliament, on the merits of which he had been consulted. The first home of the Museum was 1 Craig Court, Charing Cross, 1837; the second, 28 Jermyn Street, 1851; the third and present home, Exhibition Road, South Kensington, on a site purchased by Government from the Commissioners.

Geology was the first of the sciences to receive Government support, because the Geological Survey was an appendix to the official Ordnance Survey; and as the work of the Geological Survey proceeded, it was strengthened by teaching not only in geology, but in chemistry, palaeontology (fossils) and zoology. To serve and enlarge the field-work of the Survey, the School of Mines was instituted; and, as noted above, its centre was the Museum of Practical Geology opened by Prince Albert on 12 May 1851, with the directive 'to apply their results to the development of the immense mineral riches granted by the bounty of Providence to our isles and their numerous colonial dependencies'. This purpose was a part of the purpose of the Great Exhibition itself: and its title, Museum of Practical Geology, testifies to it. The Natural History Museum has a geological department as one of its main parts. The Geological Museum concentrates on geology, combining practical with theoretical requirements.

The long separation of the departments in South Kensington from those in Jermyn Street imposed a strain. But the Geological Survey of 1835-1935 suffered a second strain of a more pleasing order. Dean Coleman of Toronto, the *doyen* of geological science in Canada, at the opening ceremony of the new museum said:

Great Britain includes but a small part of the earth's surface as compared with some other countries, but how many sides of geology are represented in its rocky structure, and how much of our knowledge of the science is due to workers within its borders.[1]

Because of the excellence of its staff and their rich experience at home, the Survey lost some of its most brilliant men to other countries, to undertake similar work there. Canada in Mount Logan commemorates W. E. Logan, the Scotsman, Montreal-born and Edinburgh-trained, who after survey work in South Wales returned to Canada to found the Geological Survey of Canada. The British Association (Ipswich, 1851) thought so highly of his paper that they printed it in full.

As we pass through our public and private galleries of painting and sculpture, we feel sometimes that we have bought more than we have made, great as our own painting record is. In the Science Museums the feeling is the other way. In invention we were inferior to none; and in so far as the specimens came from overseas, they were, by and large, an epitome of the British Empire and its maritime enterprise.

NATURAL HISTORY MUSEUM

This takes us back to the origins of museums, so well defined by Dr Johnson as 'a repository of learned curiosities'. The museum idea began with the University building erected at Alexandria by Ptolemy Soter, *c.*280 B.C. Our museum history began with Sir Hans Sloane, who bequeathed to the State for £20,000 (the original cost having exceeded £50,000) his collections of natural history, largely built up from the West Indies. Hans Sloane, 1660-1753, was of Chelsea: Sloane Square and Hans Place (adjoining Harrods) commemorate him. In 1754 trustees purchased Montague House and placed in it the Sloane collections, together with the Cottonian collection and Harleian MSS.— hence the British Museum. In 1806 Antiquities and Coins were separated from Natural History, which latter was expanded by the addition of new branches, notably botany, based on the collections of Sir Joseph Banks. In 1857 the modern British Museum, with its great circular reading room, was

[1] Sir John Smith Fleet, *The First Hundred Years of the Geological Survey of Great Britain* (1937), p. 205.

constructed. But the Royal Commission on Scientific Instruction (1871-5) reported that the Natural History part suffered from acute congestion, and advised its removal. The Government thereupon built the present Natural History Museum on the site of the 1862 Exhibition, granted by the 1851 Commissioners (architect, Alfred Waterhouse). It was handed over to the Trustees of the British Museum in 1880, and the collections were transferred, 1880-2, from Bloomsbury.

SCIENCE MUSEUM

Least of all does this museum tell us by its title what we shall find there. It is in the main a museum of mechanical science. Historically, it is an offshoot of the South Kensington Museum, of which it was an original part. In the old South Kensington there were collections of foods, animal products, building materials and educational apparatus, together with a Patent Museum of mechanical inventions which belonged to the Commissioners of Patents. I quote at this point an official typescript:

In 1864 a collection of Naval Models and Marine Engines, consisting mainly of ship models, was lent by the Admiralty, and by 1873 when the models belonging to the Admiralty were transferred to Greenwich, there remained a large number of important objects sufficient to form an interesting collection illustrating ship and boat construction and marine engineering. This has been continually extended until today it is one of the most important collections of its kind in existence.

In 1874 the Royal Commission on Scientific Instruction drew attention to the desirability of forming a collection of Physical and Mechanical instruments, and this was commenced in the following year. The Loan Exhibition of Scientific Instruments and Apparatus, which was held at South Kensington in 1876, gave a great impetus to the scheme, and many objects there shown were secured for the Museum, with the result that a most instructive collection of scientific apparatus and instruments was built up.

In 1884 the contents of the Patent Museum were transferred to the Science Museum greatly extending its scope and in effect advancing it from a mere teaching collection of the Royal College of Science to the standing of a National Museum of applied Science.

In 1910 the need of more adequate accommodation for the Science Museum was fully realised, and an influential and representative deputation of leaders in science and industry waited upon the President of the Board of Education to lay before him their views of the importance of developing the Science Museum and of providing more ample accommodation for the collections. In the following year the President of the Board appointed a Departmental Committee, of which Sir Hugh Bell, Bart., was Chairman, to enquire into the Science Museum, its organisation, its aims and its requirements. It reported in 1912, and it is from this time that the Museum in its present form, and with its present aims, really dates.

The Science Museum is stated to be the only *national* museum of science in the country. Its library of 300,000 titles, to which, of course, students of the Imperial College have access, can compare with any science library in Europe.[1] But the visiting youth of Britain will remember the Museum by such things as George Stephenson's 'Rocket' and the model of the Orville Wright aeroplane. The original of this was here for some years, but recently has been returned with ceremony to the U.S.A. in accordance with the wish expressed in the will of Orville Wright, who died in 1948. At the same time the first jet engine, designed by Sir Frank Whittle, who flew the first jet plane, was presented to the Minister of Supply by 'Power Jets Limited', and is now in the Museum.

IMPERIAL INSTITUTE

If imperial economy had developed along the lines widely expected in 1887, the Imperial Institute might have become a focal point of educational activity, conducted on an imperial level and embracing on equal terms Great Britain, the Dominions and the colonies. But this aim has been only partially realized if by 'imperial' we mean a combination of equal-ranking nations, as the Imperial College of Science and Technology combines the royal colleges.

Built by subscription (to which the Indian Princes contributed handsomely) on a splendid central site given by the Commissioners at a nominal rent, it nevertheless found itself unable to finance its activities. Therefore the British

---

[1] The Library of the Science Museum was built up with the Museum, but to it the students of the Imperial College have ready access because it is housed in their domain, the entrance to it facing the Imperial Institute's main entrance.

Government took it over and vested its control in the Colonial Secretary, the United Kingdom supporting it, with help also from Governments overseas. But after World War I there was no federal authority representing equally the United Kingdom, India, the Dominions, and the Colonies; and therefore after the Imperial Economic Conference of 1923 it was vested (1925) in the Department of Overseas Trade. This was a makeshift and ran the risk of lowering the Institute to an appendage of Empire marketing. Nevertheless, before and during World War II valuable research was conducted on Empire products (plant and animal as well as mineral), especially for India, and contacts were developed with schools and school teachers. Continuing this trend, the Commonwealth Scientific Conference of 1946 recommended that the scientific work be transferred to the Colonial Secretary and the educational work to the Minister of Education. This division of tasks is now in being; and with co-operation from the Dominions the Institute is able, *inter alia*, 'to carry on its task of making the overseas Empire better known to schools of England and Wales through its Exhibition Galleries, its Panel of Empire Lectures and its visual aids to Commonwealth knowledge'.

Along the west side of the Institute building now runs the newly opened Canadian Exhibition, equipped with all the devices of which the New World is a master; along the east side runs the Indian section of the Imperial Institute, while above this, and approached independently, is the Indian section of the Victoria and Albert Museum. But the centre of the Institute, which is the centre of the whole estate, is an imperial void. It is no more than an administrative convenience for the University of London and other bodies requiring a large examination hall; and its central approach, as at present utilized, with one entrance for male candidates and another for female, is about as inspiring as the exterior of a labour exchange.

If one thinks of the idea in the Prince Consort's mind—and his was the master mind which designed the whole—this central space in this central site surely should have a distinctive function. I can think of nothing more fitting than a great school of anthropology and sociology, of primitive man and civilized man, with a world sweep that is at once imperial, and international.

In the British Commonwealth with its diversity of peoples and many problems of mixed economy there is a magnificent field for research. Here the descendants of Thomas Huxley and Herbert Spencer—old friends—could join hands and out-buckle Buckle in their contribution to the history of civilization. Unfortunately at the moment this does not appear practicable.

We have now completed our short tour of South Kensington. The estate, we see, presents a peculiar jumble of planning and accretion. Yet behind it all we can still see the grand design of Prince Albert and Henry Cole and give credit to the profits of the Great Exhibition which made it possible. And if we look further with the eye of imagination, can we not see behind the Victorian buildings of South Kensington the shining glass structure of the original Palace standing in Hyde Park close by, the marvels it contained, and the millions from all countries who came to visit and admire?

APPENDIX I

THE GREAT EXHIBITION[1]

ON Saturday the Great Exhibition closed its wonderful career, and the public took their last farewell of its splendours. After being open for five months and 11 days and concentrating in that time a larger amount of admiration than has probably ever been given within the same period to the works of man, the pageant terminates, the doors of the Crystal Palace no longer yield to the open sesame of money, and in a few days hence thousands of hands will be busily engaged in removing all those triumphs of human skill, and those evidences of natural wealth which the world was assembled to behold. It was natural that such an event should be regarded by all who witnessed it with no ordinary degree of emotion. Feelings of gratified curiosity, of national pride, and of enthusiasm at the public homage paid to industrial pursuits, were tempered with regret that a spectacle so grand and unique should ever have a termination. The ephemeral existence assigned to the Exhibition has all along been fully recognized, yet it was impossible that so marvellous an undertaking could run its brief career without gathering around it many attachments, sympathies, and associations which at the last it proved difficult to sever. Each person who had visited the building had found therein some objects that, by appealing to his imagination or his tastes, had gradually grown into favourites. With a large proportion it was the edifice itself which took the firmest hold upon their hearts. Its vastness, its simplicity and regularity of structural details, and a certain atmosphere of mysterious grandeur which pervades it, are features which harmonize so perfectly with our character as a people, that they must have left a strong impression. If the whole country does not now protest against the wanton and aimless destruction of the Crystal Palace we shall be very much surprised. It is only when we are about to lose them that we begin to find the value of objects which have insensibly become endeared to us. As with the building, so it was also with many of the works of art, the treasures of wealth, and the examples of ingenuity which it contained. The "Amazon," Van der Ven's "Eve," Strazza's "Ishmael," the two French bronzes,

[1] From *The Times* of Monday 13 October 1851.

126

and many other contributions of the highest artistic merit were, for the last time, to be gazed at by the admiring multitude. All who have wondered over the *chef d'œuvres* of Sevres and the Gobelins, who, in Tunis had spent pleasant hours in examining everything, from the richly brocaded dresses to the tent hung with wild beasts' skins; or who in India had feasted their eyes on the splendid evidences of an ancient civilization—all had to take a final farewell of what had interested and moved them so strongly. The mechanical wonders of the place were about to be withdrawn from public view. The card-making machine, the circular wool-comb, Appold's pump, and Whitworth's tools, were to be seen no longer. The gratuitous distribution of envelopes and soda water was to cease, and the alarm bedsteads were to do duty before admiring groups of chambermaids and cooks no longer. Even the time of that king of diamonds, the Koh-i-noor, was up; and, after having attracted more curiosity and inflicted more disappointment than anything of its size ever did since the world was created, the period had arrived when it must cease to shine its best before the public. Under such circumstances, and with the mingled feelings which they could not help suggesting, the crowds of half-crown visitors bent their way to the Crystal Palace on Saturday. The weather was splendid, and the sun looked down warmly upon the only great building in the world, which does not inhospitably exclude his rays. At 9 o'clock visitors began to arrive, and they continued to pour in steadily almost until the closing-bells had commenced to ring. All who came remained to the last and, although the numbers present were not so great as some had anticipated, they rose higher than on any previous half-crown day, and were amply sufficient to make the death scene of the Exhibition worthy of its unprecedented popularity. There were 53,061 visitors altogether, and as might have been expected, they busied themselves during the entire day in examining once more all the objects which on former occasions had chiefly attracted their interest. Some few were strangers taking at one view their first and last look of a spectacle which in grandeur they may not hope soon to see equalled. There was also a slight sprinkling of the humbler orders present, and among them a band of hop-pickers with wreaths of the plant around their hats. In the main, however, the assemblage belonged to the middle and wealthier classes, and consisted of *habitués* of the Exhibition, or, at least, of people who had been there several times before. Faces that had not been seen in the interior since the first month after the opening were recognized among the crowd, and it was evident that every rank and grade of society was fairly represented upon an occasion interesting alike to all. An eager desire was manifested, especially in the French department, to purchase mementos of the great display, and, in consequence, everything but an open sale was in progress. As the day wore on, a remarkable concentration of people in the nave began to be discernible. The side avenues and courts were deserted, and from end to end of the building nothing was to be seen but a great sea of human beings filling up the centre, and agitated by a thousand different currents of curiosity, which kept the mass in motion without progress. Time passed, and the circulation in the transept became rather impeded. The people seemed to be taking up their position there, and the galleries, as far as the eye could reach, were occupied by spectators, who, as they gazed on the vast assemblage beneath, evidently appeared to expect that some public demonstration was about to be made. The organs, which had been played constantly during the early part of the day, were now silent, and even that wonderful man Herr Sommer, with his still more wonderful instrument, sent forth no longer those astonishing volumes of sound which have rendered him, *par excellence*, the trumpeter of the Exhibition. Nothing was to be heard but that strange and mysterious hum of voices which, rising from all large assemblages, is imposing, but which in the Crystal Palace, swelling upwards from more than 50,000 people, leaves an impression upon the mind not soon to be forgotten. It was drawing near 5 o'clock, from the top of Keith and Co.'s Spitalfields silk trophy, the whole nave, east and west, the area of the transept, and the galleries might be seen packed with a dense mass of black hats, through which at intervals a struggling female bonnet emerged here and there into light. The vast multitude had now become stationary, and were evidently awaiting, in silent but intense excitement, the last act of a great event, immortal in the annals of the 19th century. It was a most solemn and affecting scene such as has rarely been witnessed, and for which an opportunity cannot soon again arise. Words cannot do it justice, and fail utterly to convey the mystery and the grandeur thus embodied to the eye. Let the reader fancy what it must have been to comprehend within one glance 50,000 people assembled under one roof in a fairy palace with walls of iron and glass, the strongest and the most fragile materials happily and splendidly combined. Let him, if he can, picture to himself that assemblage in the centre of that edifice filled with specimens of human industry and natural wealth, from every civilized community and the remotest corners of the globe. Let him tax his imagination to the uttermost, and still beyond the material magnificence of the spectacle presented to him—let him remember that the stream of life on which he looks down contains in it the intellect and the heart of the greatest metropolis and the most powerful empire in the world—that strong feelings, such as rarely find utterance in a form so sublime, are about to find expression from that multitude, and that in heathen times, even when liberty was still a new power upon the earth, the voice of the people was held to be the voice of God. Not only the days, but the minutes of the Great Exhibition were numbered, and the first sign of its dissolution was given by Osler's crystal fountain. Just before 5 o'clock struck the feathery jet of water from its summit suddenly ceased, and the silence of the vast assemblage became deeper and more intense. The moment at last came. Mr. Belshaw appeared at the west corner of the transept-gallery on the south side, bearing a large red flag in his hand. This he displayed as the clock struck, and instantly all the organs in the building were hurling into the air the well-known notes of the National Anthem. At the same moment the assembled multitudes uncovered; and those who witnessed this act of loyalty from an advantageous position will long remember the effect which it produced upon their minds. Where just before nothing was visible but a mass of black hats stretching away until lost in the distance, immediately there appeared a great sea of up-turned animated faces, and to the solemn silence of expectancy succeeded a volume of sound in which the voices of the people were heartily joined. The Crystal Palace is not adapted for organ music, and, notwithstanding the number of them exhibited, they cannot, from the size of the building, be played in concert. The consequence was that, as a musical performance,—there being no proper organization in the matter,—the singing of "God save the Queen" was a very discordant demonstration of loyalty. Herr Sommer did everything in his power and in that of his instrument to keep the people in tune, but he was only partially successful. Some professional singers also gave their aid upon the occasion, and inspired the assemblage with courage to follow. On the whole, however, foreigners would have managed this matter better; and, though it is useless now to express regrets, it does seem a pity that proper steps were not taken to make the performance of the National Anthem as effective as it might have been. About the feeling which accompanied it there could be no mistake, for as soon as it had closed there arose such cheers as Englishmen alone know how to give. These were continued for several minutes, and when the last of them died away there passed over the entire building, and with an effect truly sublime, a tremendous rolling sound, like that of thunder, caused by thousands of feet stamping their loyalty upon the boarded floors. Under this demonstration every part of the edifice trembled, and, as it swept from west to east, many an eye was raised with anxiety to the girders and pillars, which in long perspective were stretched out before them.

And now the time had arrived for the death peal of the Exhibition to be rung out. Some one hung out from the gallery of the transept a piece of calico, on which was inscribed the well-known passage from Shakspeare's

Tempest, &c.:—

> "Our revels now are ended: these our actors,
> "As I foretold you, were all spirits, and
> "Are melted into air, into thin air;
> "And, like the baseless fabric of this vision,
> "The cloud-capped towers, the gorgeous palaces,
> "The solemn temples, the great globe itself,—
> "Yea, all which it inherit, shall dissolve,
> "And, like this unsubstantial pageant faded,
> "Leave not a rack behind."

A minute or two was allowed to elapse before the fatal signal was given, and during this brief interval the assemblage remained silent and motionless. At last it came, and a perfect storm of bell peals broke over the building. The executive seemed to have collected all their strength for a last effort in this department of their duties, and we do hope that to the other statistics of the great undertaking now closed may at once be added the number of tympanums broken on the final day. Ireland, with her characteristic love of making as much noise as possible with the tongue, has sent the most powerful bells to the Exhibition, but these resources, added to the bells of all nations, were deemed insufficient, and China had to come to the rescue with her gongs, and India to strike up some fine savage notes from her tom-toms, before the signs of an intention to depart were unmistakeably manifested. The concourse of people for a long time remained massed together, as if no power could separate or fuse them; but at last small currents and ripples of human beings might be seen setting towards the exit-doors, and these gradually increased in volume and rapidity as the shades of evening fell. One by one the gaslamps were lighted, and the building, divided between the empire of day and night, assumed an aspect curiously in harmony with its defunct character. The crowds flowed out faster every minute, and first the western, and then the eastern portions of the nave, began to show vacant spaces. In the meantime, the ringing of the bells was occasionally suspended, and in the intervals hearty cheers were given for Prince Albert, for the Prince of Wales, for Mr. Paxton, for Mr. Fox, for the exhibitors, and upon various other grounds. An attempt, too, was made by some vocalists to get up a musical performance, but their efforts were instantly drowned by the revived energies of the ringers. Some one proposed a cheer for Kossuth, but it met with no response, except some derisive laughter. The galleries and the eastern and western naves had now been completely cleared, but a dense body still clung round the crystal fountain, many filling bottles with water from it as a memento, and others struggling in vain to approach it for that purpose. The police and the Sappers appeared on the scene, first in small knots and then, when they had moved the people on a little, in extended line. By gently pressing on them they at last induced them to go, but it was dark, and half-past 6 o'clock, before the building was completely cleared, and the bells finally ceased tolling. The Executive Committee, and the chief members of their staff, met in the transept when it was all over, and many and hearty were the congratulations which they exchanged on the happy termination of their brilliant labours. It is rarely, indeed, that a body of men have assembled at the close of any undertaking with more legitimate grounds for feeling pleasure and satisfaction. The Great Exhibition has been mainly the work of their hands, and its triumphant success is naturally regarded by them as their highest reward. Even the Sappers participated in the gratification which the event of Saturday inspired, and before the building was left to silence and solitude they made its dim and shadowy interior ring with three hearty cheers for the Queen.

In looking back over the career of the vast enterprise which has thus auspiciously been terminated, the consideration which first and most strongly impresses itself on the mind is the unprecedented popularity which it has attracted. Of this we quote some striking facts as illustrations. In the month of May 734,782 visits were paid to the building; in June, 1,133,116; in July, 1,314,176; in August, 1,023,435; in September, 1,155,240; and in the first 11 days of October, 841,107. These figures give a total of 6,201,856 as the sum of visits to the Exhibition. Every one will calculate according to his particular fancy the proportion between visits and visitors, but at least it is obvious that several millions of people have had their minds enlarged, and their respect for industrial pursuits increased, by a portion of their time, more or less considerable, being spent in the Crystal Palace. The greatest number of people ascertained to have been in the building at any one time was at 2 o'clock on Tuesday last, when 92,000 persons were present. On the same day the number of visitors reached its *maximum*, and was 109,915. Between 11 and 12 o'clock on Monday last 28,853 persons entered the building in one hour. When it is remembered that these extraordinary figures, which can be thoroughly relied on for accuracy, illustrate popular movements that only a few years ago would have been pronounced on the highest authority most dangerous to the safety of the State, we have the more reason to wonder that they should have taken place not only without disorder, but also almost without crime. The total number of charges made at the police-station at the Prince of Wales' Gate relating to offences within the building is, we are informed, 25, of which nine were for picking pockets, six for attempts to do so, and ten for petty larcenies at stalls. Such facts speak for themselves, and certainly constitute it as one of the proudest boasts connected with the Exhibition that property worth millions of money should have been inspected during nearly half-a-year by millions of people belonging to every class and grade of society, with only a few trifling crimes, involving no article of any value. From this agreeable feature connected with the popularity of the Crystal Palace we pass to another still more so. Shortly after the opening, the Executive Committee had the question of admitting charitable institutions gratuitously pressed upon their notice, and they decided not to do so, upon grounds which perhaps at the time were thought hard and unfeeling.—What was the result? An immense spring of private benevolence, which has not been confined to the metropolis or its neighbourhood, but has extended to every part of England, and the influence of which, passing from the very poor to the struggling independence of the country, has induced masters to send their servants, manufacturers their hands, bankers and merchants their clerks, tradesmen their apprentices, railway companies their men, and last, most wanted and most common of all, induced the owners and occupiers of the soil to send up, by subscription among them, their agricultural labourers. From a return with which we have been favoured by Mr. W. Murray, we extract some remarkable facts with reference to the attendance of charity and other schools at the Exhibition. It appears that up to the 9th of July, when he took charge of that department, no record was kept of the schools that came, and Mr. Murray can only ascertain an authentic list of 21, giving a total of 4,093 children. By the return, 466 schools have visited the building, and of these Christ's Hospital sent the largest number, amounting to 900. On the 14th of July there were 15 schools present, and 1,300 children; on the 30th, 13, and on the 6th of August, 19. On the 21st, 15 schools and 1,022 children; on the 18th of September, 33 schools and 2,729 children; on the 25th, 18 schools and 1,374 children; on the 2nd of October, 25 schools and 1,427 children; on the 8th of October, 23 schools and 1,312 children. The return includes a list of 23 parties, chiefly agricultural labourers, and including 7,758 persons sent up from the country by private benevolence. Such results are exceedingly gratifying, and will throw an additional lustre round the memory of the Great Exhibition. Looking at the popularity of the undertaking in a monetary point of view, the facts are equally extraordinary. The largest amount taken at the doors on any of the 5s. days was 5,078*l*., on the 24th of May. The greatest half-crown day was Saturday last, when 4,845*l*. 13s. 6d. was received. The greatest shilling day was Tuesday last, when the sum taken amounted to 5,283*l*. 3s. In May the highest receipts were on the 24th, when upwards of 5,000*l*. was taken, the lowest being the pound days. In June the greatest was a shilling day, when upwards of 3,000*l*. was taken; the lowest being the first shilling day. In July, the highest (a half-crown day) was the 18th, when nearly 4,000*l.* was received; the lowest being the 19th, a 5s. day. During the month of August the harvest operations told visibly on the receipts, the greatest being on the 5th, a shilling day, when more than 3,000*l.* was taken, and the lowest being on the 2d and the 30th. During the month of September the average take was still smaller, but the 29th and 30th were great shilling days, and brought in 3,000*l.* each. These *data* satisfactorily establish not only the vast success of the Exhibition, in a pecuniary point of view, but the constant and untiring assiduity with which the country, according to its ability, has come to visit and be instructed by the great spectacle. It is curious to remark that, whether the admission fee was 5s., 2s. 6d., or 1s., while the number of visitors fluctuated accordingly, the actual sums taken under circumstances of similar excitement were nearly equal. This, if it proves nothing else, seems to indicate that the Royal Commission adopted a judicious scale of charges. From the facts thus recorded the popularity of the Exhibition is placed in a position beyond dispute or question. The people flocked to it with an enthusiasm unprecedented in the annals of public spectacles, and, besides contributing to its grandeur by their presence, they have thrown around its brief but brilliant career the halo of an extended benevolence and the charm of a singular immunity from crime.

While they have thus rendered homage at the shrine of industry, it is satisfactory to think that no means have been neglected for preserving and rendering permanent the lessons of experience which the Exhibition teaches, the lights for future guidance which it discloses, the wants which it develops, and the theoretic truths which it illustrates. Of no public event that has ever happened do such complete records exist. From these, speculative·minds will hereafter be able to abstract their full significance; but it is now, while curiosity and interest are still awake on the whole subject, and while the closing stimulates these faculties in an unwonted degree, that the full importance is appreciated of giving a practical aim and direction to those vague impressions of wonder which the survey of so many objects leaves behind. Men, in this country at least, do not rest satisfied with sentimental results, and if the doctrines of universal brotherhood and of a new starting point to industry were the only general conclusions that they had to fall back upon, we fear that they might come in a very short time to think lightly enough of the Great Exhibition. The two great issues raised by the event which has just terminated may be briefly stated thus:— In what direction as an industrial community should we henceforth travel, and by what means should we proceed? Should we, yielding to those tastes for the splendid, which the possession of great wealth promotes, dedicate our efforts to the costly and the beautiful in production,—or should our course be still guided by those unpretending and material influences which have already raised us to such a pitch of prosperity and power? Standing between the civilization of the New World and that of the Old, should we raise our manufactures to the highest European and Oriental standards of taste, or should we still struggle chiefly to extend their boundaries and to command, by the element of price, the markets of the world? That is one issue, and is already receiving a solution by which we may hope in time to secure both the alternatives suggested, and to show that, practically, they may be united in the same industrial system. The reports of the juries, the association of such men as Mr. Redgrave, Mr. Cole, Mr. Owen Jones, and Mr. Pugin, for the selection of objects on which to found a pure school of design, the labours of Mr. Digby Wyatt and others in the same direction; and above all, the project of the Society of Arts for the establishment of elementary drawing schools,—these and other influences, added to the impetus which the public mind has already received on the subject, must tend greatly to raise the character of our art manufactures. On the other hand, the mortifying but useful defeats which we have received from our children across the Atlantic, the wide publicity given to new materials, machines, and processes—the certainty of an improved patent law in the next session of Parliament, and, above all, the opportunities which (notwithstanding an unfortunate decision of the Royal Commission) have been afforded by the display just terminated for observing how far price affects the prosperity of trade,—these and other considerations will keep our manufactures utilitarian in their character, and strengthen vastly the mechanical and inventive genius of the country. The second issue which the Exhibition raises, viz., how best we should proceed in the industrial career which lies before us, has hitherto been chiefly dealt with in the various schemes for the appropriation of the surplus. Some think that we must effect a radical change in our educational system—that we must substitute living science for dead literature, and distribute the honours and rewards of life in channels where they may fructify to the use of the commonwealth instead of being limited to the learned professions, the military and naval services, and the residents of our universities. To others this seems a slow and doubtful process. They advocate therefore the principle of association as the best for securing industrial progress. They say, bring the leading men in manufactures, commerce, and science into close and intimate communication with each other,—establish an intelligent supervision of every branch of production by those most interested and likely to be best informed,—have annual reports made in each department, and let the whole world be invited to assist in carrying forward the vast scheme of human labour which has hitherto been prosecuted at random and without any knowledge or appreciation of the system which pervaded it. The public must eventually decide this contest of opinions, and their verdict, whichever alternative it inclines to, or whether or not it embraces both, will not only determine one of the most important questions that the Exhibition has raised, but prove fraught with the gravest consequences to the welfare of this country and of mankind at large.[1]

[1] *The Times*, in its allusion to the Sappers (our Royal Engineers) on pp. 130-1, might have added that they discharged to perfection their difficult task of fire-prevention; and that so satisfied were exhibitors with the precautions of the Executive Committee of the Exhibition that they deemed it unnecessary to incur the fire premium of 1 per cent asked by the insurance companies.

APPENDIX II

THIS Appendix contains a number of documents from the Royal Archives, mainly from the series of volumes F 24-28. A number of others have been utilized in the text. Vol. F 24 contains correspondence up to August 1851, F 25 from 10 August 1851 to 5 March 1858; F 26 consists of printed matter. F 27 covers the period from 17 September 1858 to 18 May 1862, and F 28 that from 22 May 1862 to 24 November 1889. These volumes, which concern closely the Royal Family, are part of the much larger series of 1851 Exhibition records.

The fact that a Royal Commission was in Cole's mind before July 1849 is brought out in his letter to Colonel Phipps:

CARLTON RIDE, 3 July 1849

My dear Sir

Herewith I send the form of a Commission which appears likely to answer the end of promoting the large periodic exhibitions. I have consulted several persons and several forms of Commissions, but I think the Fine Arts Commission is on the whole the best precedent. As a Commission of Inquiry, I believe it will be perfectly efficacious.

If the draft should appear to H.R.H. the Prince suitable, then I learn that the proper course would be for you to write privately to Sir George Grey on the subject, and conveying H.R.H.'s wishes. If no obstacles present themselves, then of course the Commissioners named must be consulted as to their willingness to serve. It is thought that an intimation of H.R.H.'s wishes should be conveyed by you as well as Sir Geo Grey. In case any obstacles should present themselves perhaps it might be expedient to ask Sir George Grey to communicate with some of us on the subject before coming to any decision, but I apprehend none will arise.

I enclose a copy of the State Paper Commission, which is a Commission of

Action—dependent on the Treasury for Funds. It seems upon inquiry that there can be no difficulties to prevent the Society of Arts from undertaking the collection of funds for this object perfectly within the scope of its Charter. And it appears that the whole responsibility in this matter will be with the Society independent of the Commission.

I have to be at the Society of Arts on Monday evening and excepting that day, I shall be ready to attend any summons to Osborne.[1]

Provincial hesitations are reflected in letters from Stafford Northcote and from Grey to Phipps. Northcote (writing from the Board of Trade) reports that Labouchere, finding Manchester in alarm at some of the proceedings of the Society of Arts, has told the Mayor that the Prince will receive them in person 'at the Palace'. Grey writes to Phipps that provincial mayors 'are surprisingly unanimous against free admission to the working classes on the no better ground than the very selfish one that the London artizans will profit more largely by such indulgence than those from a distance'. Birmingham and Glasgow are 'obstinate in their opinion that money will not be wanted'. Again, Grey to Phipps (1 April 1850): 'People are ready enough to take hold of any excuse for not paying their money. However, if the Manchester guarantee of £25,000 was a *bona fide* one, it would at least secure you against the possibility of failure for want of money.'[2]

The Prince's fondness for detail is illustrated by several documents:

The Prince to Lord John Russell[3]   BUCKINGHAM PALACE, 2 *July* 1850

Lord S's[4] objection to the softness of the soil will not hold for May, June, July, the months during which the riding would take place. And as to hurdling, the Office of Woods must have quantities in store. If not, however, they are quickly and easily procured and could even be hired for a couple of months. There is a quantity of Wattle Hurdles in St. James's Park, which ought, on grounds of

---

[1] Royal Archives: Exhibition of 1851, vol. F8.

[2] All these are from vol. F24

[3] After Lord Seymour from Woods and Forests had opposed the provision of a temporary ride in Kensington Gardens to compensate the inconvenience arising from the Exhibition.

[4] Edward Adolphus Seymour, 12th Duke of Somerset, 1804-85, 1st Commissioner of Works, with seat in Cabinet 1851-2. He had been made 1st Commissioner of Woods and Forests, 15 April 1850, and the office was reorganized in 1851.

economy, one day to be changed for Iron Hurdles and I am sure will be so. Could the Iron Hurdles not be used first for Kensington and then transferred to St. James's Park? I hope you will ask Ld Palmerston to say a few words in debate on the communications with foreign governments and the disappointment that they would justly feel at the overthrow of the Exhibition at the 11th hour.[1]

Again on 25 September 1861, anent the newly opened Horticultural Gardens:

H.R.H. has not observed at Railway Stations, or at certain places in London where exhibitions of all sorts are advertised in large letters, that any such means have been taken to make the existence of these gardens known to the public, and such a mode of advertisement is probably more effectual and less expensive than that of notices in the newspapers.[1]

A letter from the Bishop of London on the provision of divine service for foreign visitors indicates the interest of the Church:

The Church Exhibition C^{ee} will continue their labours and have other measures under consideration for promoting the spiritual welfare of our visitors and for preventing or lessening the moral evils to which large heterogeneous assemblages are peculiarly exposed.

A number of documents touched on the controversies about the admission of the public:[1]

Granville to Grey   BOARD OF TRADE, 17 *January* 1851

I met Macaulay and Dickens yesterday at Ld John's. The latter (D) thought we ought not to delay too long the shilling admissions, and Macaulay made a regular speech on the necessity of admitting on the 1st day, whatever you did afterwards, at 1/-. ... With respect to the Queen's visits to the Exhibition, it must be remembered that it is very likely that tho' it may be possible to admit visitors, the arrangements will not be complete on the first of May. ... We propose having a meeting of the Finance Committee and of a *formal* Commission on Tuesday, to approve of Mr. Cubitt being entrusted with the arrangements to supply steam power to the machinery in accordance with the promise of the Commissioners.

[1] Vol. F 24.

Grey remonstrates with Paxton (23 January 1851) for writing to the press in favour of free admissions.[1]

Granville to Grey   *24 January* 1851

Paxton's head has been turned by the events of the last six months, and it is not surprising that they should have had that effect upon a self-educated man . . . .

I hear that Lord Overstone says that he will take the first opportunity of publicly stating his opinion in favour of Parliament paying for everything. The guarantee has had the same effect on his head, as the building on that of Paxton. I hope he will not do what he says, as he will cover himself with ridicule.

Vol. F25 contains documents about the political difficulties facing the Prince's South Kensington plans:

Memorandum of 1856 by the Prince on the site of the National Gallery

Notes that in 1852 the Government of Lord Derby voted £150,000 to supplement the £150,000 of the Commissioners.

In 1853 the Gov^t of Ld Aberdeen got a further vote, to complete the purchase, and the House of Commons Committee recommended the Kensington site for the National Gallery.

Now (1856) Ld Elcho, with *The Times* behind him, wishes to refer the issue to a Royal Commission.

Palmerston agrees with the Queen's indignation at *The Times*, but 'there is something to be said against the proposed site at Kensington Gore, on account of its distance from the inhabited and frequented parts of the Metropolis'.

                                                                 27 June 1856

Viscount Palmerston regrets to say that Lord Elcho's address for a Commission to enquire and report, as to the site of the National Gallery, was carried by a majority of 8 (153-145). The Opposers of the motion had infinitely the best of the debate.

---

[1] This refers to an open letter from Joseph Paxton to the Rt Hon. Lord John Russell— Shall there be free admission to the Glass Palace? He argued for free admission, except at the start and on Wednesdays. With gratuitous admission there would be a flowing stream of people: whereas with exacted payment visitors would become fixtures from morning to night. Therefore he asked for a Parliamentary grant. The psychology of the letter is interesting, impetuous, impatient of profit and loss, captivated with the idea of flow—the flowing stream of humanity and the breaking down of barriers: the tide that sweeps to victory.

Lord Broughton (John Cam Hobhouse) now wrote to Grey and enclosed the Report of the National Gallery Commission of 13 July 1857.[1]

Three to one, one not voting, were in favour of the present site, as being 'more accessible and more familiar'. The Commissioners in the order of their signatures were Broughton, H. H. Milman, M. Faraday, C. R. Cockerell, Geo. Richmond. The Secretary was H. Montagu Butler (the future Master of Trinity, Cambridge).

Disraeli[2] to the Prince   *5 March* 1858

I need not assure yr. R.H. that I have never, for a moment, in or out of office, swerved from those views which yr. R.H. deigned to develop to me, when I first had the honor of being placed in confidential relations to yr. R.H. and the entire fulfilment of which I believe to be alike necessary to the intellectual progress and the material prosperity of this country.

It was proposed that the Commissioners should now refund to the Government its share in the purchase money. The Prince was anxious that the money thus refunded should be earmarked for 'the National Buildings for the Departments of Science and Art'. This, said Disraeli, won't do: it is not a genuine repayment. But the Kensington Estate Bill passed the Commons, 25 January 1858, 'after a sharp ordeal'.

The controversies begun in the lifetime of the Prince Consort continued after his death, and are reflected in several documents of vol. F 28.

There is a letter from his secretary, Charles Grey, to Disraeli soliciting support for South Kensington:

It is for the purchase by Gov[t] on the most favourable terms of the Buildings erected for the late Exhibition [*sc.* of 1862], and of the site on which they stand. The Site consists of something over 16 acres, and the total cost of the purchase and of the accommodation therein of the British Museum Natural History Collection, the Patent Museum, the School of Geology from Jermyn Street, and the National Portrait Gallery, would be less than the estimate for last year's scheme.

[1] 'No report at all', was the Prince's disgusted comment.
[2] The Earl of Derby is Premier once more, and Disraeli at the Exchequer.

The Commissioners could sell the 16 acres 'to much better advantage to speculators'. But pursuant to the views of the Prince Consort, they prefer to sell the land to Government for this purpose at below cost, the price asked being sufficient to pay off the mortgages, etc.

To this Disraeli replies:

My dear General [*sc*. Grey]   GROSVENOR GATE, 15 *May* 1863

You may always rely upon my utmost exertions as a Royal Commissioner of 1851 to carry into effect the plans of our beloved and illustrious chief.

Ever yours sincerely,

B. DISRAELI

Lord Henry Lennox to Grey

I have just seen Disraeli, and we are taking every possible step to induce our men to vote right. The Prince of Wales should say he is for it.

Lennox to Grey   H. OF C., 2 *July*, 11 *p.m.*

While I write, the impression is quite universal that the Gov^t will be beaten and that the Building will not be voted.

If so, the result will be mainly attributable to the Chancellor of the Exchequer [*sc*. Gladstone] for the miserable way in which he introduced the vote. I never heard anything more clumsy or *fatal*. I said a few words, but it was difficult to speak in the face of so hostile an audience.

By the assertion that the Contractors were *not* bound to remove the buildings from the land now belonging to Govt, Gladstone raised up a host of enemies, and the cry that the land had been bought under false pretences was freely alluded to. I know not what may be the result, but I can testify that Disraeli has done his best. . . .

P.S. The danger is so great that Northcote was put up to make an amendment, which might save the Govt. He was howled down. Disraeli has tried to come to the rescue, but all in vain. The uproar is very great.

Disraeli to Grey

Before I go to bed—

A crushing defeat! The House was really mad or drunk. It began badly. Gladstone made much too clever a speech and sarcastic instead of conciliating. . . . I sent to Gladstone not to divide—but he insisted. 'Tis most vexatious. I kept away nearly 70 men. However, we have got the land! That's something and we may yet accomplish all we wished and more than we have hoped.

Lennox to Grey

After Gladstone's speech, all hope was gone.

WINDSOR CASTLE, 3 *July* 1863

The Queen much regrets the vote of last night, and fears Ld Palmerston's unavoidable absence had much to do with it. However we have got the land, and we must now not lose a moment in preparing plans and estimates for the necessary building to replace the present Exhibition one. . . .

Palmerston to the Queen [a frank and sensible letter]

Gladstone was unfortunate in his speech, it was futile to say that he and those who agree with him are the only people who know anything of the matter. The fact is that there is strong prejudice against the Building. . . . The great array of opponents consisted of artists and architects who had little or no share in planning and erecting the building and who of course expect that their Body Corporate will obtain employment and reap honor and fame from the erection of the Building to be substituted for the present one. . . . All parties were bent on its going.

Lastly, from vol. F 28 some correspondence dealing with the decline and fall of Henry Cole:

Ponsonby to the Queen

Cole wants to come and fume about South Kensington against Mr. Lowe [i.e. against the plan of Robert Lowe, Chancellor of the Exchequer 1868-73].

It appears that Mr. Cole has hitherto exercised despotic power at South Kensington. . . . He has always had his own way. The Gov^t (some of them) object to this and wish to place the Museum under the trustees of the British Museum.

Newscutting

Mr. Cole resigns, and Ld Sandon informs Mr. Mundella [A. J. Mundella, some-time vice-president of the Committee of Council for Education] that steps will be taken to bring the various departments in South Kensington into more direct relations with the Education Department in which they will virtually be merged.

In 1876, with the conservatives in office, the Duke of Richmond explains to the Queen the proposed changes: 'Mr Owen. to be Director of the (*sc.* Natural History) Museum—the post held by Mr. Cole, when he was secretary.' The Queen (still writing on deep mourning paper) assents: this is what her dear husband would have liked.

Mr Cole (now Sir Henry Cole, K.C.B., 1875) submits a pamphlet with map of the main square of the South Kensington estate: north, Kensington Road; south, Cromwell Road; east, Exhibition Road; west, Prince Albert Road; and in the square, reading from north to south, the Albert Hall, the Royal Horticultural Society's Garden, and the site of the Exhibition of 1862 (allotted for the Natural History Museum).

APPENDIX III

THE PRINCE'S MODEL LODGING

Correspondence between Prince Albert and the Duke of Wellington

THE PRINCE'S MODEL LODGING

[The lodging to-day is in Kennington Park. It faces Kennington Road and a plate explains that the building was originally designed by the Prince Consort in 1851 and altered in 1898. It is now an office for the Park staff. It was built for two families, with an outside stone staircase leading to the upper lodging (now enclosed). The concrete ceiling and the hollow bricks of the walls are strong and good.]

Royal Archives: vol. F 24, No. 66

The Prince to the Duke of Wellington

As President of the Society for the improvement of the Condition of the labouring Classes, & taking much interest in the subject, I have been anxious that a Model Lodging house should be erected in connection with & as part of the Exhibition.

It has been found impossible to have this erected within the space allotted in Hyde Park for the Exhibition Building—nor after the objections taken to the introduction of brick & mortar into the Park can it be placed with any propriety in any other situation within the limits of the Park itself.

It has, however, been suggested to me that it might without inconvenience be erected in the vacant ground belonging to the Cavalry Barracks—and that if it were placed a short distance back from the line of the enclosure wall which runs parallel to the Exhibition building, & if about 50 feet of that wall were taken down, a separate approach might be given to it, without in any way interfering with the Barracks—

Whether this is so or not, I cannot at present pretend to say—But should no objection appear to the use of this site, I should be prepared to have the house erected at my own expence, & afterwards, either removed, or given over to the Ordnance for the use of the Barracks. As affording accommodation to six Married Soldiers & their Families it might probably be desirable to retain it.

As it rests entirely with your Grace as Commander in Chief, & with the M. Genl of the Ordnance to decide whether or not this piece of ground shall be so appropriated, I have not allowed any steps to be taken in the matter till your sanction shall be obtained, & an Official Report made on the subject by the proper Officers—

But that your Grace may know what is proposed, I send you herewith a design for the Elevation as also a ground Plan of the proposed building.

Should your Grace approve of what is suggested perhaps you will have the goodness to forward my letter & the enclosures for the information of Lord Anglesey, whose concurrence will also be necessary.

F 24, No. 74

The Duke of Wellington to the Prince

Field Marshal the Duke of Wellington will take means that Your Royal Highness may have as soon as possible an exact plan and dimensions of the ground not occupied by Buildings at the Hyde Park Barracks! and he recommends to Your Royal Highness to write to the Master General of the Ordnance if Your Royal

Highness should desire to occupy any part of the ground with a building for the purpose of the Great Exhibition of 1851!

If the Master General should entertain any doubt for a moment respecting the appropriation of the ground to any purpose not strictly military, he will refer to the Officer who commands the Army in Chief!

The Case will then be in it's regular course, and the Commander in Chief will give such opinion to the Master General as may be consistent with propriety!

All of which is submitted to Your Royal Highness by Your Royal Highness' most devoted Servant etc.

F 24, No. 74

The Duke of Wellington to the Prince   LONDON, 25 *January* 1851

Field Marshal the Duke of Wellington presents his duty to Your Royal Highness. He received at midnight last night Your Royal Highness' commands in relation to a building to be constructed on the ground belonging to the Barracks in Hyde Park.

F.M. the Duke of Wellington has been on the ground this morning.

There appears no ground on which any building can be placed excepting a sort of yard in which is the Riding House and the Stabling of the Officers' Horses and he observed that these buildings did not exceed in Height the inclosing Wall on the Knights' bridge Road.

He has a perfect recollection of the desire frequently expressed that an addition should be made to Buildings at this Barrack of an Hospital for the sick of the Regiment there quartered. The Hospital at present in use being considered unhealthy.

It appears to Field Marshal the Duke of Wellington that an additional building for the use of Married Soldiers will not be required at the Barrack in Hyde Park; unless required at the same time for the Barrack in the Regents Park; and likewise for the Cavalry Barrack at Windsor occupied in Rotation by the two Cuirassier Reg^ts of Life Guards; and by the Reg^t of Horse Guards Blue.

F 24, No. 75

The Duke of Wellington to the Prince   LONDON, 27 *January* 1851

Field Marshal the Duke of Wellington presents his duty to Your Royal Highness. He incloses the Report and Sketch received of the ground at the Horse Barracks in Hyde Park, and the site proposed for the Building which Your Royal Highness wishes to be erected.

Your Royal Highness will see that besides the consent of the Master General of the Ordnance that this building should be erected on the ground belonging to the Barracks, it will be necessary to have the consent of the Commissioners of Woods and Forests to the construction of any Building on this ground of which the Height sh. exceed that of the Surrounding Boundary Walls. vz. ten feet.

F.M. the Duke of Wellington concludes that the objections to the Height of the Building are founded on the complaints of the owners and occupiers of Houses on the opposite side of the Turnpike Road from London to Kens'gton.

Your Royal Highness will be able to determine after examination of the proposed Plans, whether Your Royal Highness will proceed farther!

The first step will be to obtain the consent of the Master General of the Ordnance to erect the Building on the ground belonging to the Ordnance: the next the consent of the Commissioners of Woods and Forests to erect a Building of which the Height sh. be eighteen feet Higher than the Surrounding Boundary Walls of the Premises.

Which is humbly submitted to Your Royal Highness by Your Royal Highness's most devoted Servant etc.

It appears that Your Royal Highness must already have the information, which these papers might afford as Mr. Roberts the Architect had been over the ground with the Officer of Engineers employed by the Ordnance.

APPENDIX IV

THE SITE OF THE CRYSTAL PALACE IN HYDE PARK

THE site of the Crystal Palace was in the large open space on the south side of Hyde Park between Rotten Row and the Kensington Road. It stretched from the present bowling green (W) to opposite the Hyde Park Barracks Riding School (E): and in winter is readily recognisable by the football pitches on the oblong of grass.

The main entrance was on the south side, facing the Prince's Gate. There is negative evidence in Crown Land Records to show that the Gate was named, not after the Prince of Wales of the day (the future King Edward VII) but after an earlier prince, possibly the Prince Regent.

The concrete foundations still remain under the site, but though uncovered in part by excavations during World War II, no marks were made by which their exact location can be identified. However, File 16757 of Crown Land Records contains a plan dated 1850, showing Hyde Park and in dotted lines the position of the building that became the Crystal Palace. When the plan of this building is superimposed on a modern Ordnance Survey sheet, its position agrees exactly with the description given in the foregoing paragraph.

INDEX I

GENERAL

INDEX II

EXHIBITS BY COMMODITY